Advancing Organizational Theory in a Complex World

T0313136

While research in organizational studies has become increasingly rich and complex, organization researchers are constantly challenged by the growing quest for theoretical advancement and innovation. To conduct theoretically rigorous and innovative research, contemporary researchers and students must develop in-depth understanding of the theoretical traditions and future prospects of their discipline. This book provides a collection of cutting-edge research topics in the field of organization and management and offers advanced research findings that explore the frontiers of the field.

Advancing Organizational Theory in a Complex World aims to provide deep insights into many influential organizational theories, including contingency theory, institutional theory, stewardship theory, population ecology theory, ambidexterity, and complexity theory. All these theories have been developed to explain the external and internal factors that influence organizational survival and evolvement. We focus on these theories because they represent some of the most important entryways into the modern literature, counterpoints to the modern literature, and a breath of fresh air to some theories that should be better known. This book shows the fruitfulness and the continuous vitality of the theoretical field of organizational studies in a critical and innovative way.

Finally, this book is dedicated to Professor Lex Donaldson, who is a thought leader in the field. The field owed this book to Lex for his lifelong dedication to organizational studies and for his creation and advancement of theories that have inspired several generations of researchers.

Jane XJ Qiu is a Senior Lecturer in the School of Management at UNSW Australia Business School, Sydney, Australia.

Ben Nanfeng Luo is an Assistant Professor in the School of Labor and Human Resources at Renmin University of China, Beijing, China.

Chris Jackson is a Professor in the School of Management at UNSW Australia Business School, Sydney, Australia.

Karin Sanders is the Head of School of Management and Professor of Organizational Behavior and Human Resource Management at UNSW Australia Business School, Sydney, Australia.

Routledge Studies in Management, Organizations and Society

For a full list of titles in this series, please visit www.routledge.com

This series presents innovative work grounded in new realities, addressing issues crucial to an understanding of the contemporary world. This is the world of organized societies, where boundaries between formal and informal, public and private, local and global organizations have been displaced or have vanished, along with other nineteenth century dichotomies and oppositions. Management, apart from becoming a specialized profession for a growing number of people, is an everyday activity for most members of modern societies.

Similarly, at the level of inquiry, culture and technology, and literature and economics, can no longer be conceived as isolated intellectual fields; conventional canons and established mainstreams are contested. Management, Organizations and Society addresses these contemporary dynamics of transformation in a manner that transcends disciplinary boundaries with books that will appeal to researchers, students, and practitioners alike.

Advancing Organizational Theory in a Complex World

Edited by Jane XJ Qiu,
Ben Nanfeng Luo, Chris Jackson,
and Karin Sanders

Routledge
Taylor & Francis Group

LONDON AND NEW YORK

First published 2017 by Routledge

2 Park Square, Milton Park, Abingdon, Oxfordshire OX14 4RN
711 Third Avenue, New York, NY 10017

Routledge is an imprint of the Taylor & Francis Group, an informa business

First issued in paperback 2018

Copyright © 2017 Taylor & Francis

Library of Congress Cataloging-in-Publication Data
CIP data has been applied for.

ISBN: 978-1-138-93557-0 (hbk)
ISBN: 978-1-138-61678-3 (pbk)

Typeset in Sabon
by Apex CoVantage, LLC

In admiration of an academic life well lived
for
Emeritus Professor Lex Donaldson BSc PhD DSc

Contents

Figures and Tables

Figures

Tables

Contributors

Andrew Binns, Executive Fellow, Center for Future Organization, Drucker School of Management, Claremont University, CA, USA

Richard M. Burton, Professor Emeritus, Fuqua School of Business, Duke University, Durham, NC, USA

Lex Donaldson, Emeritus Professor, School of Management, UNSW Australia Business School, Sydney

William Egelhoff, Professor Emeritus, School of Management Systems, Fordham Graduate School of Business, New York

Dorthe D. Håkonsson, Professor, Department of Business Development and Technology and Interdisciplinary Center for Organizational Architecture, Business and Social Sciences, Aarhus University, Denmark

Markus A. Höllerer, Professor, Department of Management, WU Vienna University of Economics and Business; Senior Scholar, School of Management, UNSW Australia Business School, Sydney

Hokyu Hwang, Senior Lecturer, School of Management, UNSW Australia Business School, Sydney

Chris Jackson, Professor, School of Management, UNSW Australia Business School, Sydney

Peter Klaas, Interdisciplinary Center for Organizational Architecture, School of Business, Aarhus University, Aarhus, Denmark; WTT A/S, Brande, Denmark

Jørgen T. Lauridsen, Professor, Department of Business and Economics, University of Southern Denmark, Odense, Denmark

Jaco Lok, Associate Head of School, School of Management, UNSW Australia Business School, Sydney

Ben Nanfeng Luo, Assistant Professor, School of Labor and Human Resources, Renmin University of China, Beijing

Børge Obel, Professor, Department of Management, and Director, Interdisciplinary Center for Organizational Architecture, Business and Social Sciences, Aarhus University, Denmark

Jane XJ Qiu, Senior Lecturer, School of Management, UNSW Australia Business School, Sydney

Karin Sanders, Head of School of Management, Professor of Organizational Behavior and Human Resource Management, UNSW Australia Business School, Sydney

Charles Snow, Professor Emeritus, Smeal College of Business, Pennsylvania State University, State College, PA, USA

Michael Tushman, Professor, Harvard Business School, Harvard University, Cambridge, MA, USA

Joachim Wolf, Professor, Institute of Business, Christian-Albrechts-University, Kiel, Germany

Kangkang Yu, Assistant Professor, School of Agricultural Economics and Rural Development, Renmin University of China, Beijing

Lex Donaldson, Colleague

The Lex Donaldson we know is quiet and reserved, not a person who trumpets his ideas and opinions. In his 2005 autobiographical article, however, Lex is both forthcoming and candid in describing his upbringing, values, and philosophy regarding social science research.

During his childhood days at nondenominational Protestant state schools, Lex learned to say what he believed to be the truth, even if it provoked controversy. He also learned that the best knowledge is scientific knowledge, and he became a strong and consistent voice in the organization sciences for positivism, functionalism, and determinism, as well as what today is referred to as contingency theory. Lex believes in quantification, control, and empiricism, and he is skeptical of theory and paradigm proliferation. Within the discipline of organization theory, Lex believes that theory should be based on the reality of organizations—observed facts interpreted and explained with validated theory.

Lex has, with his significant books and articles, become an important and well-recognized voice in the organizational sciences, and especially in the area of organization design. His views have shaped the debate and development of contingency theory in organization design and have helped the field to advance.

Given his background and belief system, it is easy to see why we wanted Lex to be a member of the Organizational Design Community (www.org designcomm.com). Established in 2010, ODC is the product of a series of international organization design workshops held annually in Denmark during 2005–09. Lex faithfully attended these workshops—traveling all the way from Australia to offer his latest thinking. Lex is one of 17 international scholars who are the founding members of ODC.

Lex is an outstanding colleague. In his teaching and academic presentations, he is clear and constructive in his comments to PhD students and faculty colleagues, and he is tolerant (but challenging!) of alternative views of organizational theory and research. If you want to debate Lex about theories of organization or about how to do social science research, you had better be prepared, because Lex's beliefs and opinions are well thought out and defensible. We have witnessed many such debates, and we believe that through these and other forums, Lex has contributed immensely to the progress of the field of organization design.

It has been our distinct pleasure to know Lex personally and to follow his work. We look forward to his future contributions in retirement.

Børge Obel and Charles Snow

Introduction

*Jane XJ Qiu, Ben Nanfeng Luo,
Chris Jackson, and Karin Sanders*

Research in organizational theory has become increasingly rich and complex. Organization theory researchers are constantly challenged by the growing quest for theoretical advancement and innovation. To conduct theoretically rigorous and innovative research, contemporary researchers and students must develop in-depth understanding of the theoretical traditions and future prospects of their discipline.

This book provides a collection of cutting-edge research topics in the field of organization and management and offers advanced research findings. The authors explore the frontiers of organizational theory by (1) critically reflecting on existing theories and advancing these theories to explain organizational phenomena better, (2) engaging in debates between different theories, (3) seeking connection and synergy between different theories, and (4) applying organizational theories in various contexts of strategic management, international business, and corporate governance.

Scholars have joined us from around the world, including Australia, China, Denmark, Germany, and the United States, in this exciting endeavor to celebrate the remarkable career of Professor Lex Donaldson, a thought leader in the field. We dedicate this book to Lex for his lifelong commitment to organizational theory research and for his creation and advancement of theories that have inspired several generations of researchers.

Those of us who know Lex understand why so many prestigious authors wanted to get together to write this book. He has always worked at the leading edge of contingency theory. Lex began his pioneering work into contingency theory with the Aston University group of British organizational researchers. He went on to develop, test, and defend contingency theory while also integrating diverse strands of research into a unified theory. This work, as well as his other work in stewardship and agency theories, for example, has been published in 8 books and over 50 articles, many of which are in top journals, such as *Academy of Management Review* and *Organization Science*. Such is his impact that he has over 14,000 citations, and his research has inspired generations of scholars across the world. Professionally, Lex has influenced managers and practitioners internationally with his views on pressing managerial issues, such as corporate governance, through his books, which have been translated into Dutch, German, and Spanish.

A few remarks about Lex personally should be offered at this point. Most of his career has been spent at the University of New South Wales, Sydney, Australia. In fact, he has been at UNSW for a remarkable 39 years. While intensely rational and intellectual, he is first and foremost an English gentleman. For example, he will always fight vociferously for what is right while at the same time being deeply caring and nurturing with colleagues. English gentlemen should also be a little quirky, and Lex is no exception: he is well-known for his strong sense of humor, love of meat sandwiches (as long as there are no vegetables inside them), and his retro use of a paper diary.

The authors of this book aim to provide deep insights into many influential organizational theories, including contingency theory, transaction costs theory, institutional theory, stewardship theory, and ambidexterity. All these theories have been developed to explain the external and internal factors that influence organizational effectiveness and legitimacy. The first three chapters examine the concept of "fit" that is key to the contingency theory of organizational design and take it to a higher level of theoretical complexity. In the first chapter, Richard M. Burton, Børge Obel, and Dorthe D. Håkonsson focus on new developments in the concept of fit for new organizational forms by examining internal and external agreements and different types of contracts as building blocks for new integrated forms. In the next chapter, Peter Klaas and Jørgen T. Lauridsen examine the process of structural adaptation to contingencies, such as organizational size and strategy, which underlies a large body of research in the Structural Adaptation to Regain Fit (SARFIT) model. In the following chapter, Ben Nanfeng Luo, Lex Donaldson, and Kangkang Yu extend the concept of structure needed to fit a single contingency to the situation where a structure needs to fit multiple contingencies. They examine the competing views of equifinality and the contingency imperative regarding the number of fitting structures.

The next chapter by Andrew Binns and Michael Tushman develops the more complex contingency concept of ambidexterity and provides a better understanding of how firms "get started" with ambidexterity. In the subsequent chapter, Jane XJ Qiu and Lex Donaldson develop structural contingency theory in an international business setting by re-examining the conventional assumption that a matrix structure is multi-hierarchical. They propose a different view: a matrix structure in an MNC is mainly a single hierarchy. Based on this new view, a quantitative model is developed to estimate the amount of "matrix advantage."

The chapter by William Egelhoff and Joachim Wolf explores how contingency theory can make organization theory more relevant to today's organizational problems. It argues that more focus on developing higher-level contingency theories of organizational functioning and design can potentially reconcile and integrate disconnected or competing lower-level theories.

The penultimate chapter by Jaco Lok, Hokyu Hwang, and Markus A. Höllerer demonstrates how to use institutional theory creatively to advance our understanding of stewardship theory. It reviews two competing theories in corporate governance—agency theory and stewardship theory—and discusses their impact from an institutional theory perspective. In the final chapter, Lex Donaldson summarizes the aforementioned chapters, reflects on the past developments of the field, and provides new thoughts for its future.

Built on the foundation laid by Lex's seminal work, this book presents new advancements in the theories that represent some of the most important entryways into the modern literature, counterpoints to that modern literature, and a breath of fresh air from theories that should be better known. We hope that this book is useful to researchers and students, especially when they are searching for, or further reflecting on, the theoretical foundations of their research in organizations. We are confident that the field of organizational theory awaits further exciting future discoveries through research and vigorous debate.

1 Contingency Theory, Dynamic Fit, and Contracts

Richard M. Burton, Børge Obel, and Dorthe D. Håkonsson[1]

Introduction

One of the most important concepts in organization theory is the concept of fit. Donaldson (2001) defines fit as a match "between the organization structure and contingency factors that has a positive effect on performance." (pp. 7–10) Building on the notion of uncertainty and its consequences, Galbraith (1974) describes fit in information processing terms: fit is a match between the demand for information processing and the capacity for information processing. This reasoning derives from Ashby's Law of Requisite Variety, which states that the variety of the organization must exceed the variety of the environment.

Burton, Obel, and Håkonsson (2015, 64) characterize the environment by its degree of complexity and uncertainty. Environmental complexity is the number of factors in the environment and their interdependency. Environmental uncertainty or unpredictability is lack of understanding or ignorance of the environment in terms of the nature of the factors and their variance.

In the multi-contingency theory (Burton et al. 2015), there are 14 factors that should be in fit, including environment, structure, incentives, and external agreements or contracts. Luo, Donaldson, and Yu (see chapter 3) analyze multiple contingencies in comparison to equifinality. Qiu and Donaldson (see chapter 5) examine the limited advantage of the matrix structure.

Despite the fact that most environments are dynamic, the emphasis has been on static fit in a static equilibrium sense (Burton and Obel 2013). Dynamic fit extends the concept of fit to include time and makes fit path dependent. Dynamic fit is the continual matching of the environment with the organizational design where the shorter the time to adjust is preferred (Nissen and Burton 2011). Klaas and Donaldson (2009), Klaas, Lauridsen, and Håkonsson (2006), and Luo and Donaldson (2013) introduced the concept over-fit and under-fit using information processing as a compensating mechanism. In a dynamic fit perspective, the organization may over time fluctuate between under-fit and over-fit. The organization desires to minimize the opportunity loss of being out of fit over time. With time included, the notion of opportunity loss is defined as the loss in performance over the time the organization is not realizing its goals—the greater the performance deviation, the greater the opportunity loss; the longer the time duration, the greater the opportunity loss (Burton and Obel 2013).

In contingency theory, an organization's boundary is a statement of what is *inside* the organization and what is *outside*. Traditionally, ownership and rent appropriation as well as property rights and derivative authority rights would define the organizational boundary (Gibbons 2005, 207). This definition, however, becomes ambiguous with outsourcing of activities and services and temporary employees. Organizational boundaries have also become more ambiguous with respect to people and activities because of user-driven innovation and similar activities (Baldwin 2012; Burton 2013; Tushman, Lakhani, and Lifshitz-Assaf 2012).

Contracts extend the managerial boundary of organizations beyond the usual property rights concepts. That is, the coordination question of "who is to do what" goes beyond ownership to include activities both inside and outside traditional boundaries to realize high performance (Baligh and Burton 1982). With ambiguous boundaries, management activities and employees often do not follow the rules of the hierarchy, but are more based on contracts that cross the traditional organizational boundary of property rights and authority (Burton et al. 2015). Thus contracts often serve as organizational coordination mechanisms, as they help specify "who is to do what when"—basic questions of organizing. This makes contracts an integral part of contingency theory of organization design.

The chapter proceeds as follows: First, we provide a review and overview of the three main types of contracts that the paper will explore: relational, agile, and formal. Next, we develop that the performance of the organization depends upon the fit of contracts with the organizational environment. We develop this argument based on information processing arguments.

Background Review of Contracts

In their seminal work "Theory of the Firm: Managerial Behavior, Agency Costs and Ownership Structure," Jensen and Meckling (1979) characterize the firm as a nexus of contracts. Jensen and Meckling took their point of departure in the theory of agency, the theory of property rights, and the theory of finance to develop a theory of the ownership structure of the firm. However, Holmström and Roberts (1998, 75) argue that contracts are much more than property rights to establish boundaries; they are also mechanisms for coordination and motivation. Hence contracts are both a mechanism to enhance optimal governance and safeguarding, as well as a mechanism to achieve coordination and adaptation (Schepker, Oh, Martynov, and Poppo 2014).

Contracts are then central to how we organize firms and a basic factor in contingency theory. In particular, contracts and environments are closely related, as contracts specify what is inside and outside the firm. Contracts always involve a quid pro quo between two entities. Contracts are frequently defined in terms of contrast: complete/incomplete, formal/relational, explicit/implicit, formal/informal, agile/non-agile, flexible/rigid, resource based/performance based, blueprint specified/design and build, fixed cost/variable cost, cost plus/fixed cost, fixed outcomes/best effort, standard/unique, and waterfall or planned sequence/one time, among other names and definitions. Each contract could be put on a continuum on these dimensions, e.g., complete to incomplete.

At the fundamental level, contracts have varying degrees of specificity: complete and incomplete. A complete contract defines everything about the exchange between the two contracting parties: what is to be done and what is the payment, both in detail. An incomplete contract is one that does not spell out everything in the exchange, e.g., marriage as the future is not known at the time of the contract. Complete and incomplete can be viewed as discrete and different, but also along a continuum of degree of incompleteness. In this sense, all contracts are incomplete to some extent.

In all contracts, there are three phases: the contract agreement process, the execution of the contracts, and the completion and payment of the contract—the ex ante and ex post, if you will. It is a time-related and path-dependent dynamic process where what is known is different at the various stages.

Grossman and Hart (1986) and Gibbons (2005), among others, divide contracts into formal and relational contracts. Formal contracts involve agreements between two parties, which involve a transaction or exchange that can be adjudicated by a court or third party. Examples include an activity of a new building according to a blueprint for a fixed fee or a professional athlete will play for a given team one year for a fixed amount of money. These contracts are specified ex ante and can be assessed ex post. The building either is in accord with the blueprint or it is not. The professional athlete either plays according to his or her contract or not. A relational contract is a contract whose effect is based upon a relationship of trust between the parties. The explicit terms of the contract are just an outline, as there are implicit terms and understandings that determine the behavior of the parties. Normally, a relational contract does not involve a court or third party for adjudication. These are sometimes called informal contracts, implicit contracts, incomplete contracts, or understood agreements, among others. These contracts can be efficient and self-enforcing and ongoing for years. They can be for minor issues, such as "I agree to watch your desk for the next 15 minutes," or "high-level diplomatic understanding" following a largely unspecified agreement. Relational contracts are frequently incomplete because of a lack of information about the future and involve trust (Uzzi 1997), but they can also be open to misunderstandings, which can lead to disagreement without recourse. Despite their ubiquity, the "enforcement" of relational contracts is problematic. If there is no enforcement, why not take advantage of the agreement? One approach is to take time into consideration and to think of relational contracts as a repeated game (Baker,

Gibbons, and Murphy 2002). That is, the parties are likely to have ongoing relational contracts for which understanding and trust will continue to be important. In the prisoner's dilemma, there is the self-interest incentive to default if the game is played one time, but if the game is repeated many times, both parties can win by cooperating over time and not defaulting (Axelrod 1987). In our experience in everyday life, we have many continuing relational contracts of understanding and trust.

Macneil's legal relational contract theory is complementary, but not identical to our development here. In the legal relational contract theory (Macneil 1980), relational contracts are discussed mainly as long-term contracts, often incomplete and more difficult to negotiate—basically they are used for more complex projects and for long-term relationships (e.g., long-term, buyer-supplier contract). They are then contrasted against discreet contracts—short term, one time, complete, easier, or non-negotiated (e.g., buying milk in a supermarket). Except for simple transactions, the complete contract is an end-point fiction; relational contracts rely upon Macneil's nine behavioral norms: role integrity; mutuality; implementation of planning; effectuation of consent; flexibility; contractual solidarity; linking norms of restitution, reliance, and expectation interest; creation and restraint of power; and harmonization with social matrix (Macneil 1980, 40). We argue that the contracting parties have limited information, are bounded rationally, and are interested in continuing relations also.

Formal and relational contracts deal with dynamic issues in different ways. A formal contract has detailed specification of activities ex ante; e.g., the design specifications for a bridge are detailed. Ex post, the bridge can be assessed to whether it meets the ex ante specifications or not. Further, a third party or court can adjudicate any deficiencies and who is responsible for correction. There can be both real and opportunity losses from non-compliance. Resources are required to fix a bridge that does not meet the specifications; opportunity losses are incurred as the use of the bridge is delayed, and, further, all of these non-contract activities take time.

For a relational contract, ex ante specifications are incomplete and ambiguous because there is uncertainty about the future or the information is not available, e.g., customer needs or demands are not known. Many possible products and services are included here: software and IT projects, research projects, and temporary specialists, among others. Even ex post, the completion of the contract can also lack specificity, which can be resolved through negotiation. However, there can also be a breakdown, and the two parties choose to part ways. For either impossibility or time and cost, no third party or court is utilized. On the other hand, the two parties may agree that the contract was completed successfully. Looking forward, as in a repeated game, the two parties may engage again in a similar contract. This establishes the relational enforcement.

Another type of contractual relationship is the agile contract. Pioneered in IT project management, agile contracts are frequently preferred to traditional contracts, such as fixed-fee contracts. An agile contract is defined in Wikipedia as follows:

> In Agile contracts, the supplier and the customer together define their common assumptions in terms of the business value, implementation risks, expenses (effort) and costs. On the basis of these assumptions, an indicative fixed price scope is agreed upon which is not yet contractually binding. This is followed by the test phase (checkpoint phase), during which the actual implementation begins. At the end of this phase, both parties compare the empirical findings with their initial assumptions. Together, they then decide on the implementation of the entire project and fixate the conditions under which changes are allowed to happen.

In short, agile is an organizational process with a series of contracts. It is a way to reduce the uncertainty and risk for both parties (Cyert and March 1963). The agile process begins with an understanding of business value, costs, and risks. Yet there is not sufficient information to specify a formal or complete contract in detail. Uncertainty is dealt with as a sequence of short-term agreements (Cyert and March 1963). A series of fixed contracts is developed to move the project along toward completion. Thus each party is not subject to over-commitment with large risk. In brief, this sequence of short-term contracts requires understanding and perhaps trust to deal with the lack of information and uncertainty. In his relational contract theory, Macneil (1980) emphasizes the need for "flexibility" (p. 50), "implementation of planning and effectuation of consent" (pp. 59–60), and relations norms of role integrity, preservation of the relation, and harmonization of relational conflict (pp. 64–68).

In a relational contract or an agile contract, incentives are a critical issue. First, the issue of what is in each player's interest has to be considered. Generally, we assume an individual wants to maximize her or his return, which may mean that the other individual is less well off. But it is possible to cooperate and both individuals win. Second, there may be a short-run opportunistic incentive where information distortion can benefit one player without the other player ever knowing (Burton and Obel 1988; Williamson 1975). The agile contracting process is a series of contracts under uncertainty, which limits the possible loss where a longer-term contract may involve greater risk. That is, there is a renewal of contracts, which limits loss and may build trust in the process. In contrast, the relational contract can be subject to opportunism. Relational contracts can evolve over time, much the same way as agile contracts.

Contracts must be considered dynamically in the multi-contingency theory of organizational design (Burton et al. 2015). While traditional coordination mechanisms such as structures are related to task division, task allocation, rewards, and information sharing, we include contracts between and among individuals and firms as elements of the organization's design and as part of the definition of the environment. Contracts as well create coordination mechanisms to deal with uncertain environments. Further, agile or relational contracts enable the organization to achieve dynamic fit – that is, to retain fit over time despite continuously changing environments.

Fit between the environment and the organization for good performance is fundamental in contingency theory. Along with organizational structure, contracts are part of the organization. The performance of the organization depends upon the fit of its contracts with its environment. In the next section, we develop the fit relationship in more detail using the information processing approach to organizational design.

Contracts under Environmental Complexity and Uncertainty

As stated earlier, the firm itself can be idealized as a nexus of contracts among property owners who control the firm's activities (Grossman and Hart 1986). Our focus here is not solely on contracts, but how external contracts are integral with multi-contingency theory of organization and dynamic fit.

Environmental complexity can often be assessed ex ante and thus detailed contracts can be written; further, the execution of the contracts can be monitored ex post. Thus the environmental complexity can be handled within formal contracts often with fixed payments. Uncertainty makes it more difficult to set fixed payments, and it may only be determined ex post. In this situation, a cost-plus contract may be preferred (Crocker and Reynolds 1993). If you are in a situation with high uncertainty, relational or agile contracts may be the better choice. Here the relationship between partners is important, and, further, the relationship between the partners is influenced in a perspective by the contractual setup (Abdi and Aulakh 2014).

In Table 1.1, we present a number of fit propositions based on an information processing perspective (Galbraith 1974) and supporting literature

Table 1.1 Contracts under Different Environmental Complexity and Uncertainty

		Uncertainty	
		Low	*High*
Complexity	high	*formal contracts* also complete, explicit, fixed cost, performance based, standard	*relational contracts* also incomplete, agile, informal, cost plus, best effort, waterfall, planned sequence
	low	*formal contracts* also complete, explicit, fixed cost	*agile contracts* also incomplete, implicit, informal, cost plus, waterfall, planned sequence

applying a dynamic fit view where time and opportunity loss are important. We specify the kind of contract, or contracts, appropriate for each environmental situation. Later, we also discuss the contracts from an incentive perspective both for people and activities, as a distinction between contracts for activities and contracts for people is often made (Gibbons 1998).

The axes in the table are complexity and uncertainty, following the characterization of the environment in Burton et al. (2015).

Related to complexity, Anderson and Dekker (2005) provide evidence that formal contracts are more often used when the size of the project contract is large—a large number of interrelated factors. Although there is a large number of factors, they can be specified. This takes time and effort ex ante. Introducing time, Ryall and Sampson (2009) confirm that firms tend to utilize formal contracts as they use more contracts. There is a learning-by-doing or time aspect of continuing contracting in play. There is the intuitive argument that relational and formal contracts are substitutes, but we argued earlier that they are used for different ways to deal with complexity and uncertainty.

If the environment is uncertain, a relational or an agile contract is preferred. It is difficult in this situation to write a contract that is easy to enforce, as the needed information is not at hand ex ante. Therefore, a contractual relationship that allows adjustment as the uncertainty unfolds will be required. If the complexity is low, then it is easy to establish a set of checkpoints in an agile contract setup. If the complexity is high, it may be more difficult, and thus a more relaxed contractual setup is needed (Poppo and Zenger 2002).

When the environment is uncertain with many states of nature possible in the future, even though the environment is not complex with many variables, to consider a relational or agile contract is required. From the contingency theory, this environment fits well with incentives that are bonus based and rewards according to what eventually happens (Burton et al. 2015). With the shadow of the future looming large for continuing relations, the people have less incentive to shirk duties and every reason to adjust to the reality as it occurs. Since we do not know what will happen, we can reward based upon what actually does happen. The classic agency theory situation addresses this matter where the principal can never know what the agent might have done, so it is imperative to give an incentive that rewards the outcomes rather than the process. With this information, it is not possible to write detailed contracts that state clearly what to do, as the principal does not know. Ex post, no monitor can assess whether the agent shirked or not. Here a relational contract is a good fit, as monitoring is not possible and no party can adjudicate ex post.

However, relational contracts pose the problem of why should the external contractor or person not shirk on his or her contract. There can be a large number of issues: quality of activities, as well as the quantity for activities; for the external people, there is a question of skill effort, quality of workmanship, and level of effort—all difficult and costly to monitor. So what is the incentive to give the best effort possible? The "shadow of the future," or repeated game approach, is one solution. Namely, there is a possibility of more contracts if activities go well. But if the contractor or person takes advantage, then future work and contracts are less likely. Relational as well as agile contracts provide both a means to limit the firm's downside risk and also provide an incentive for the contractor or the person to do a good job. There is a balance to be achieved. Further, there is the time dimension, as the outcome of the contract can only be observed ex post. In an empirical investigation, Carson, Madhok, and Wu (2006), using concepts of ambiguity and opportunism, found a positive relationship between ambiguity and supplier opportunism in the relational contracting regime, ceteris paribus (p. 1062). Here the shadow of the future is not sufficiently long for the contractor to forego opportunistic behavior. Nonetheless, agile contracts, which are a sequence of relational contracts, can work very well on an ongoing basis. Soili, Nari, and Jukka (2010) provide evidence for this kind of reasoning from the timber industry in Finland.

Thus relational contracts depend upon behavior in implementation, the perceived incentives and payoffs, and the development of trust over time. Agile or continuing relational contracts can continue for an extended time or can fail at any time. Nonetheless, relational contracts fit well when the uncertainty is high. The size of the contract can be an important moderator.

Since some parts of your environment may be complex while other parts may be less complex, the previous discussion states what might be a normal situation for an organization.

Formal contracts can be used to reduce uncertainty, as they create specificity and expectations to reduce uncertainties. That is, the formal contract is a control and coordination instrument (Holmström and Roberts 1998). The risk is that the formal contract may bring the wrong certainty to the situation; that is, the resulting outcome does not meet the goals. Here the relational and agile contracts are more effective, as they are adaptable to changing situations and give incentives to the people to take whatever actions are needed to meet the goals.

Poppo and Zenger (2002) find empirical support for complementarity. Managers appear to couple their increasingly customized contracts with high levels of relational governance (and vice versa). Moreover, this interdependence underlies contracts' ability to generate improvements in exchange performance. These results indicate that contracts themselves are not static in practice, but there is a learning process, which enhances the exchange process when using both formal and relational contracting.

In short, a firm should search a balance of formal contracts to reduce complexity and a sequence of relational (i.e., agile) contacts to react and hedge against uncertainty. Formal contracts are more likely for external activities, as they bring certainty of expectations—particularly for large projects; relational and agile contracts offer greater flexibility for people and timeliness for the firm. The precise balance will be firm dependent—a function of many considerations of which the contracts are a part.

Abdi and Aulakh (2014) add a nuanced consideration to the substitute-complement question by introducing moderators. They argue that environmental uncertainty (i.e., instability and unpredictability of the external environment) drives the formal and relational arrangements into a more substitutive relationship by elevating the adaptation complications in which increasing reliance on either form of governance inhibits the effective operation of the other. Contrastingly, behavioral uncertainty (in the form of inadequate common grounds and shared frameworks among collaborating firms) encumbers the understanding of partner behavior and conduct and drives the governance mechanisms into a more complementary relationship in which contractual and relational mechanisms facilitate the effective operation of each other.

In terms of our model, formal contracts could be substituted with relational contracts provided there was deep understanding between the parties. Nevertheless, the formal and relational contracts are complements to deal with complexity and uncertainty. This is consistent with the law of requisite variety (Ashby 1956). The mix of contracts must consider time and dynamic fit. The complementarity of contracts follows from a learning process between the individuals or firms. It is time that switches formal and relational contracts from a one-time substitute to a complement when there is a sequence of contracts and a longer-term relationship between the individuals or firms. It is the shadow of the future that makes the difference and explains the seeming conundrum that formal and relational contracts are not substitutes. For organizational design, this is a central insight.

Referring again to Table 1.1, we find that uncertainty is more dominant for fit than complexity. For low uncertainty, formal contracts work well; for high uncertainty, relational and agile contracts work better.

Contracts for External Activities

Contracts differentiate between *contracts for activities* and external *contracts with people* (Baker et al. 2002; Burton et al. 2015; Jensen and Meckling 1976). These types of contracts are different in a number of ways, including risk sharing and incentives. Generally, the two types of contracts are different in their content and mix of relational and formal contracts (Gibbons 1998) and the dynamic perspective by the contractual setup (Abdi and Aulakh 2014).

A *contract for activities* deals with activities that can be accomplished inside the firm but are moved to be performed outside the firm and thus to be an external activity. This is the classic make-buy decision (Hart 1995; Williamson 2008) or market-hierarchy decision (Egelhoff and Wolf, see chapter 6). External activities may require firm-specific investment, i.e., asset specificity (Williamson 1975), which introduces a risk element and the possibility of holdup in ex post adjustments. For example, Nike buys its branded shoes from suppliers who must invest in machines to make Nike shoes. These machines are limited to this activity. Nike thus outsources its core production activity. Similarly, neither Microsoft nor Apple makes its laptops or phones. There is a large amount of literature on outsourcing that gives many reasons for not having the activities inside the organization, including cost, quality, and flexibility (Larsen, Manning, and Pedersen 2013). Outsourcing can be efficient, as a firm can incur lower cost (Burton et al. 2015). On the other hand, from a dynamic-fit perspective, contracts related to outsourcing can reduce the flexibility and thus the ability to obtain dynamic fit over time. This was seen in the case of LEGO, which one year lost a major part of the Christmas sales of a new product because of an incorrect estimate of the sales potential and the lack of capability to adjust the outsourced production (Burton et al. 2015).

Contracts with External People

Regarding *contracts with people*, organizations engage individual specialists in IT, law, accounting, and strategic planning, as well as unskilled temporary individuals. These individuals usually have well-defined jobs and are supervised or report to an individual inside the firm. Often, they are hired to work on a very specific task. Sometimes, the distinction between internal and external people is difficult to observe, as firm's managers supervise both employees and external individuals, who frequently work side by side. The major distinction is the nature of the contract that the individual has with the firm—not necessarily the work that is being accomplished. Contracts with external people reduce the "after the contract" information processing demands by setting expectations for "who will do what when." Simon (1951) and March and Simon (1958) discuss the nature of the employment contract for internal people; namely, an individual gives up some freedom for direction on what to do in exchange for compensation, i.e., substitute authority for pay. External people are also subject to authority, but it is usually more narrowly defined than for an employee. At the same time, contracts also provide a more flexible boundary for the organization with the outside environment. External people make the organization more agile from a dynamic perspective since the organization can adjust its capabilities and capacities quickly to meet its needs. Therefore, the ability to obtain dynamic fit is enhanced.

Comparison of Contracts for Activities and with People

As we have argued, there is a difference between contracts related to people and contracts related to activities. One reason is that the contract between two organizations is often represented by two legal entities. Further, we have referred to external activities as those activities that normally take place outside the organization. It can be the outsourcing of production of LEGO bricks, or it can be outsourcing of the company bookkeeping. In most cases, you cannot observe the activity itself, but only the result. In these cases, we have the "traditional" principal-agency issues.

With respect to external people, the issue is slightly different as you are normally in a situation where the individuals are working inside the organization where you can observe their behaviors as well as their results. This is the case whether you have a contract with a particular individual, or an agency representing the individual. Turner (2004), in the context of project contract management, makes the distinction between whether one is buying something in the marketplace or dealing with a situation where resources are assembled in a climate of cooperation to achieve an objective. In a simplistic way, one can argue that in the case of external activities, it is a matter of safeguarding against risk, while in the case of external people, it is a matter of creating incentives toward a common goal. In both cases, the contract has uncertainty and complex relations.

The incentives for external activities are suggested to be "high powered" (Gibbons 1998, 207), as the realization of external activities requires greater commitment on the part of contractors, e.g., specific assets, and the potential opportunity loss is larger. The incentives are linked directly to the finished activity, e.g., completing the bridge according to the specifications. Crocker and Reynolds (1993) found for US Air Force contracting that formal contracts tend to mitigate opportunism and ex post difficulties, but at the expense of ex ante investment in contract specification. With effort, the information can be obtained, indicating the situation is predictable, in principle. Here the information to write a detailed contract ex ante is known; the specification of the finished activity can be specified in detail. The incentive or payoff is specific to the finished activity with direct payment, i.e., high-powered incentive. Although the activity can be very complicated and detailed, it is specified and detailed and can be adjudicated. In terms of the Ashby's Law of Requisite Variety, the contract as controller has sufficient variety for the external activity variety (Ashby 1956). In many ways, the formal contract is an ideal control, which works well in practice under complexity, but does not work well when unpredictability or uncertainty is present. However, the counterargument is that the contract itself creates its own predictable situation.

Conclusion

Fit, defined as two firm activities or elements working well together for good performance, is a fundamental concept in organizational design (Donaldson 2001). The environmental uncertainty and complexity are basic contingencies for the organizational design. Formal and relational contracts are two types of contracts that are part of the organization's definition of its environment and design (Gibbons and Henderson 2012; Grossman and Hart 1986); they also serve as mechanisms for coordination and control (Holmström and Roberts 1998). How do contracts help make these activities and people fit well with the firm?

This chapter develops the basic argument that firms can manage their boundaries by complementing traditional property rights concepts and hierarchical forms with external contracts for activities and people. Further, we have used the concept of dynamic fit where the speed of organizational adjustment to environmental changes is an important criterion. The proper choice of contracts enables firms to obtain dynamic fit over time—going beyond these traditional organizational forms.

Formal contracts work well when ex ante environmental uncertainty is low—for both low and high complexity. Relational and agile contracts work well when the environmental uncertainty is high. That is, the choice of good contracts is contingent upon the environment where uncertainty is a more important discriminator than complexity. The analysis and development of incentives to mitigate opportunism is central in this dynamic context.

Viewed from a design point of view, contracts are not only chosen to deal with uncertainty but also to reduce uncertainty by specifying what is to occur. Holmström and Roberts (1998, 75) argue that contracts are much more than property rights to establish boundaries; they are also mechanisms for coordination and motivation. Hence, contracts are both a mechanism to enhance optimal governance and safeguarding as well as an incentive for achieving coordination and adaptation (Schepker et al. 2014). Formal and relational or agile contracts are complements when time and dynamic fit are considered. Formal contracts can be used to eliminate uncertainty ex ante, but only up to a point. Relational contracts, and agile contracts, which are used in a sequence, are appropriate for dealing with uncertainty. Individuals and firms can learn to coordinate better with both types of contracts. It is a central insight that formal and relational contracts are complements when there is a shadow of the future to consider. The concept of dynamic fit where time and opportunity loss are central provides a framework to incorporate contracts into contingency theory.

In this chapter, we have extended the traditional contingency theory of organization to include contracts. In examining the environmental contingencies of complexity and uncertainty, we argue that formal, relational, and agile contracts fit better for different environments. Formal contracts work better when uncertainty is low; relational and agile contracts work better when uncertainty is high. Our understanding of contracts in contingency theory is embryonic with much yet to learn. Many questions are open. Specific hypotheses need to be developed and tested. In today's world where there is growing utilization of external activities and external people by the firm, we cannot ignore this challenge of putting contracts directly into contingency theory.

Note

1 We would like to thank Katerina Peterkova, Department of Law, Aarhus University, for valuable comments and suggestions.

References

Abdi, M. and P. S. Aulakh. 2014. Locus of uncertainty and the relationship between contractual and relational governance in cross-border interfirm relationships. *Journal of Management.* doi:10.1177/0149206314541152.

Anderson, S. W. and H. C. Dekker. 2005. Management control for market transactions: The relation between transaction characteristics, incomplete contract design, and subsequent performance. *Management Science* 51 (12):1734–52. doi:10. 1287/mnsc.1050.0456.

Ashby, W. R. 1956. *An introduction to cybernetics.* London: Methuen.

Baker, G., R. Gibbons, and K. J. Murphy. 2002. Relational contracts and the theory of the firm. *Quarterly Journal of Economics* 117 (1):39–84. doi:10.1162/ 003355302753399445.

Baldwin, C. Y. 2012. Organization design for business ecosystems. *Journal of Organization Design* 1 (1):20–23.

Baligh, H. H. and R. M. Burton. 1982. Moveable boundaries between organizations and markets. *International Journal of Policy Analysis and Information Systems* 6 (4):435–49.

Burton, R. M. 2013. The future of organization design: An interpretative synthesis in three themes. *Journal of Organization Design* 2 (1):42–4.

Burton, R. M. and B. Obel. 1988. Opportunism, incentives, and the M-form hypothesis: A laboratory study. *Journal of Economic Behavior & Organization* 10 (1): 99–119.

Burton, R. M. and B. Obel. 2013. Design rules for dynamic organization design: The contribution of computational modeling. In *Handbook of economic organization: Integrating economic and organization theory.* Grandori, Anna, ed. Cheltenham, UK: Edward Elgar Publishing, 223–44.

Burton, R. M., B. Obel, and D. D. Håkonsson. 2015. *Organizational design: A step-by-step approach.* Cambridge and New York: Cambridge University Press.

Carson, S. J., A. Madhok, and T. Wu. 2006. Uncertainty, opportunism, and governance: The effects of volatility and ambiguity on formal and relational contracting. *Academy of Management Journal* 49 (5):1058–77. doi:10.5465/amj.2006. 22798187.

Crocker, K. J. and K. J. Reynolds. 1993. The efficiency of incomplete contracts: An empirical analysis of Air Force engine procurement. *RAND Journal of Economics* 24 (1):126–46. doi:10.2307/2555956.

Cyert, R. M. and J. G. March. 1963. *A behavioral theory of the firm.* Vol. 2, Englewood Cliffs, NJ: Prentice-Hall.

Donaldson, L. 2001. *The contingency theory of organizations.* Thousand Oaks, CA: Sage.

Galbraith, J. R. 1974. Organization design: An information processing view. *Interfaces* 4 (3):28–36.

Gibbons, R. 1998. Incentives in organizations. *Journal of Economic Perspectives* 12 (4): 115–32. doi:10.1257/jep.12.4.115.

Gibbons, R. 2005. Four formal (izable) theories of the firm? *Journal of Economic Behavior & Organization* 58 (2):200–45.

Gibbons, R. and R. Henderson. 2012. Relational contracts and organizational capabilities. *Organization Science* 23 (5):1350–64.

Grossman, S. J. and O. D. Hart. 1986. The costs and benefits of ownership: A theory of vertical and lateral integration. *Journal of Political Economy* 94 (4):691–719. doi:10.2307/1833199.

Hart, O. 1995. *Firms, contracts, and financial structure: Discussion of the foundations of the incomplete contracting model*. Oxford: Oxford University Press.

Holmström, B. and J. Roberts. 1998. The boundaries of the firm revisited. *Journal of Economic Perspectives* 12 (4):73–94. doi:10.2307/2646895.

Jensen, M.C. & Meckling, W.H. (1976). Theory of the Firm: Managerial Behavior, Agency Costs and Ownership Structure. *Journal of Financial Economics* III: 305–360.

Klaas, P. and L. Donaldson. 2009. Underfits versus overfits in the contingency theory of organizational design: Asymmetric effects of misfits on performance. In *New approaches to organization design*. Bøllingtoft, A., D. D. Håkonsson, J. F. Nielsen, C. C. Snow, and J. Ulhøi, eds. New York: Springer, 147–68.

Klaas, P., J. Lauridsen, and D. D. Håkonsson. 2006. New developments in contingency fit theory. In *Organization design: The evolving state of the art*. Burton, R. M., B. Eriksen, D. D. Håkonsson, and C. C. Snow, eds. New York: Springer, 143–64.

Larsen, M. M., S. Manning, and T. Pedersen. 2013. Uncovering the hidden costs of offshoring: The interplay of complexity, organizational design, and experience. *Strategic Management Journal* 34 (5):533–52.

Luo, B. N. and L. Donaldson. 2013. Misfits in organization design: Information processing as a compensatory mechanism. *Journal of Organization Design* 2 (1):2–10.

Macneil, I. R. 1980. *The new social contract: An inquiry into modern contractual relations*. New Haven, CT: Yale University Press.

March, J. G. and H. A. Simon. 1958. *Organizations*. New York: John Wiley & Sons.

Nissen, M. E. and R. M. Burton. 2011. Designing organizations for dynamic fit: System stability, maneuverability, and opportunity loss. *IEEE Transactions on Systems, Man and Cybernetics, Part A: Systems and Humans* 41 (3):418–33.

Poppo, L. and T. Zenger. 2002. Do formal contracts and relational governance function as substitutes or complements? *Strategic Management Journal* 23 (8):707–25. doi:10.1002/smj.249.

Ryall, M. D. and R. C. Sampson. 2009. Formal contracts in the presence of relational enforcement mechanisms: Evidence from technology development projects. *Management Science* 55 (6):906–25. doi:10.1287/mnsc.1090.0995.

Schepker, D. J., W-Y. Oh, A. Martynov, and L. Poppo. 2014. The many futures of contracts moving beyond structure and safeguarding to coordination and adaptation. *Journal of Management* 40 (1):193–225.

Simon, H. A. 1951. A formal theory of the employment relationship. *Econometrica: Journal of the Econometric Society* 19 (3):293–305.

Soili, N. H., L. Nari, and L. Jukka. 2010. Flexibility in contract terms and contracting processes. *International Journal of Managing Projects in Business* 3 (3):462–78. doi:10.1108/17538371011056084.

Turner, J. R. 2004. Farsighted project contract management: Incomplete in its entirety. *Construction Management and Economics* 22 (1):75–83. doi:10.1080/01 44619042000186077.

Tushman, M., K. Lakhani, and H. Lifshitz-Assaf. 2012. Open innovation and organization design. *Journal of Organization Design* 1 (1):24–27.

Uzzi, B. 1997. Interfirm networks and the paradox of embeddedness: Social structure and economic action in the New York apparel industry. *Administrative Science Quarterly* 42 (1):35–67.

Williamson, O. E. 1975. *Markets and hierarchies*. New York: Free Press.

Williamson, O. E. 2008. Outsourcing: Transaction cost economics and supply chain management. *Journal of Supply Chain Management* 44 (2):5–16. doi:10.1111/j. 1745–493X.2008.00051.x.

2 Structural Adaptation to Regain Fit

Multiple Misfits and Structural Complexity

Peter Klaas and Jørgen T. Lauridsen

Introduction

Donaldson's (1987, 1999) Structural Adaptation to Regain Fit (SARFIT) model explains how structural adaptation is driven by the decrease in performance, or fitness, from misfits. The decrease in performance creates an incentive to remove misfits so that performance can be restored and even increased from previous levels.

The SARFIT model operates on a single fit-misfit relationship between a structural and a contingency variable. In a multi-contingency context, for SARFIT to work, it is necessary to assume that misfits can be fixed independently, one at a time in a sequential manner.

With reference to complexity, a large body of theories and studies has argued that misfits may not be independent, in which case many or all misfits must be removed before fitness is regained. In this situation, adaptation and change is revolutionary and rare rather than incremental and continuous. With complexity, SARFIT will work only by chance. In a test of their multi-contingency model, Burton et al. (2002) did not find that more misfits degraded performance more than just one misfit. With reference to complexity theory and Kaufmann's (1993) N,K model, they concluded that "rational changes in the design may or may not lead to improved performance, and may lead to large deterioration in performance" (Burton et al. 2002, 1480).

However, for SARFIT to operate in a multi-contingency setting, complexity may represent less of a problem than what first meets the eye. Constraints reduce the number of misfits that must be considered simultaneously and offer opportunities for the designer to economize on information (Alexander 1964; Arrow 1974; Ashby 1963; March and Simon 1958).

In this chapter, we revisit the unique dataset on misfit from the Burton et al. (2002) study in order to learn more about the nature of misfits in general and the potential impact from complexity and constraints on SARFIT in particular.

The chapter proceeds as follows: First, we introduce in more detail the concepts of complexity and constraints. The overall analytical framework used in this chapter is the information processing (IP) view (Galbraith 1977), and we also revisit this framework briefly. Second, we develop four hypotheses concerning complexity and constraints, and third we test the four hypotheses against the Burton et al. (2002) dataset. Fourth, we discuss and elaborate on our results. Fifth, and finally, we present our conclusions.

Theoretical Concepts

Following the interpretation of Donaldson (2001) and others, contingency theory is part of adaptive functionalism. In explaining variations in organizational structure, the emphasis on the adaptation by the organization to its environment makes structural contingency theory part of adaptive functionalism (Donaldson 1996, 63).

As a consequence, contingency theory should first and foremost be evaluated in terms of its ability to explain and predict relevant aspects of this managerial process in terms of how it is causally and statistically related to contingency, structure, and performance.

Early contingency theory focused on the performance effects from bivariate contingency—structure relationships, and this led to the identification of numerous different but largely unrelated bivariate fit relationships.

But organizations and their environments are differentiated and complex structures, and so different concepts for integrating bivariate relationships into a coherent multi-contingency model emerged. A multi-contingency model is a multidimensional constellation of conceptually distinct characteristics that commonly occur together (Meyer, Tsui, and Hinings 1993, 1175).

In this chapter, we will use the term "component" to describe conceptually distinct characteristics that commonly occur together. Such distinct characteristics, or components, have been termed in various ways in the literature, such as "contingency factors" and "properties." For example, the multi-contingency model of Burton et al. (2002) consists of a large number of components, including environment, strategy, climate, technology, size, formalization, centralization, and configuration (Burton et al. 2002, 1463).

Mutual interdependency between the components making up the configuration causes what has broadly been termed complexity and inertia. Before continuing the discussion of complexity, let us clarify what is meant by interdependency and complexity. Interdependency means that the value, or state, of one component affects the value, or state, of one or several other components; e.g., if the strategy of the organization is changed, then it will affect the structure of that organization also. For interdependency to be present between components, they must somehow be causally linked together (Alexander 1964, 108). If two components are causally linked together, we may illustrate this by connecting the two components with a line. This is illustrated in Figure 2.3 on p. 30; e.g., centralization is linked to technology so that the value of centralization is dependent on a matching value, or state, of the technology component for obtaining fit and good performance. The causality may be analyzed in terms of information processing. Information processing is a process, but there is causality between variations in IP structure and variations in IP process because IP capacity is determined structurally. If a technology represents a high demand for IP, then it will cause an overload on a highly centralized IP structure. The overload will cause delays that will ultimately cause lower performance through longer lead times, higher-quality costs, etc. In this way, there are structural and processual causal links between contingency, structure, and performance that may be analyzed with the IP framework (Arrow 1974; Galbraith 1977).

Organizations are complex systems that include multiple interdependencies at various levels (Caspin-Wagner, Lewin, Massini, and Peeters 2013, 35), and this situation is also illustrated in Figure 2.3 (p. 30). In the figure, there are nine components that are linked by eight links. In the same figure, if we imagine that all components had links to all other components, then each component would be linked to $(9 - 1) = 8$ other components. Complexity is an ambiguous concept, and we will discuss it further in the following sections. But in general, complexity has been interpreted as a function of the number of components and, in particular, the number of links between components. If there are many links between components, then interdependency is said to be high and complexity also.

In one particular interpretation, Kaufmann (1993) conceptualized complexity as a function of two numbers, N and K. N is the number of components, and K is the number of links connecting one component to the others, or, more precisely, the number of other components that the fitness contribution from one component is dependent on. In our earlier example, $N = 9$ and $K = 1$ in the first situation and $K = N - 1 = 8$ in the second.

Kaufmann's model highlights how complexity, in terms of a large K, complicates adaptation and change. In the first situation, changing the value, or state, of one component only involves considering one other component simultaneously. The fitness contribution of one component is dependent on one other component only; e.g., the fitness contribution from the state of the structural component is only dependent on the state of the strategy component. This is a simple design problem, and it corresponds to the contingency imperative situation as it is discussed by Luo et al. in their chapter in this volume. With a bivariate relationship, there are only $2! = 2$ possible combinations, and if one of them is a given, imperative value, then there is only one possible solution. But in the second situation, changing the value of one component involves the simultaneous consideration of eight other components, which makes the design problem much more complex. There exist a total of $9! = 362,880$ different solutions to the design problem, which must be considered simultaneously in each step of the design process.

There is a third situation in which the number of links between components is not constant. Components may be ordered into a hierarchy of subsystems where there are many links between the components internally in each subsystem but few links between them. For example, with nine components decomposed into three subsystems of three components each, the total number of different solutions that need to be considered simultaneously for each subsystem is 3! = 6; Simon (1962, 2002) referred to this type of design as a nearly decomposable (ND) system and argued that adaptation—irrespective of whether the process is functionalist or evolutionary—can only happen for complex systems if they are ND systems, because non-ND systems take too long to adapt successfully. For a recent discussion of interdependency, complexity, and ND systems in organization design, see also Caspin-Wagner et al. (2013).

Burton et al. (2002) specified and tested a multi-contingency model consisting of 90 bivariate misfit statements. This study is of particular interest because it focuses on misfit rather than on fit. In functional adaptation, the incentive for changing the design is the poor performance that is caused by the presence of misfits and the improvements from fixing them. Before continuing the discussion of the Burton et al. study of performance effects from misfits, let us clarify the concept of misfit and how it relates to interdependency and complexity as we apply it here. Misfit is an organizational misalignment that diminishes performance (Burton et al. 2002, 1461). The concept of misfit may be operationalized in many different ways, but a binary approach is what we will use here, since it reflects the operationalization used by Burton et al. (2002), Kaufmann (1993), Alexander (1964), and Ashby (1963). In the binary approach, for each underlying causal link between any two components, they may either be aligned or misaligned. If they are aligned, then they are in fit and misfit = 0. If they are misaligned, then misfit = 1. As an example, in Figure 2.3 (p. 30), high centralization is a misfit with a non-routine technology. In this case, misfit = 1. The misfit may be removed by changing the value, or state, of one of the components so that misfit = 0; e.g., low centralization would not be a misfit with a non-routine technology. Misfits diminish performance, and removing a misfit will cause an increase in performance. This is what SARFIT specifies. Following Alexander (1964), note that if two components are not causally linked, then they are independent on each other and the value of one will not have any performance effects depending on the value of the other.

Building from our earlier discussion of interdependency and complexity, if—as SARFIT assumes—the designer only needs to consider one misfit relationship at a time, then $K = 1$ and complexity is low even if the design comprises a larger number of components, as in the example from Figure 2.3, where $N = 9$. But, on the other hand, if interdependency and complexity is high, then with nine components, $K = 8$, and so the designer would have to remove all eight misfits simultaneously in order to improve performance in one step. Or, stated differently, if the designer changed the value, or state, in one of the components in order to remove one misfit, seven new ones would be created. In this situation, removing one misfit would not improve misfit as SARFIT claims, but, on the contrary, diminish performance even further.

This, in a nutshell, is the challenge from complexity and multi-contingency frameworks on functionalist adaptation.

Returning to the Burton et al. (2002) study on misfits, it was found that organizations without misfits performed better than those with misfits, but not that several misfits degraded performance more than fewer misfits. Departing from the concept of complexity, they refer to Kaufmann (1993) and Simon (1962) and explain that complexity is a function of the number of components, N, and the number of connections between them, K. In their model, N equals the number of misfit statements, 90, and K the number of actual misfits in the particular organization; for 1 misfit, $K = 1$, for 2, $K = 2$, etc. Burton et al. (2002) argue that in their model, an organization with misfits $K > 0$ would find it difficult to identify a combination of operating solutions (i.e., a combination that would fix all existing misfits without creating any new ones in the process) that yield good performance. They conclude that small marginal changes in the design may or may not lead to improved performance and may even lead to a large deterioration in performance. The reader should note that the Burton et al. (2002) interpretation of K is different from our conceptualization as presented earlier. Burton et al. interpret K as the number of misfits that each firm has, while we interpret K as the number of links from a misfit to other misfits, or interdependency. We chose this interpretation because it complies with the general interpretation of interdependency without compromising the analysis and conclusions of the Burton et al. study.

What is termed complexity theory emerged as a set of loosely related ideas and concepts in the late 1990s (see the *Organization Science* 1999 special issue, 10 (3)). However, complexity and its implications for open systems theory and cybernetic control was formulated already in the late 1950s. Ashby (1963), in his seminal work on cybernetic control and the law of requisite variety, noted that control (by control we mean a process of removing deviations, or misfits) in the very large systems is of particular interest, for those systems are complex and composed of an almost uncountable number of parts (Ashby 1963, 244). He continues to assert that the number of components (i.e., a large N) is irrelevant for the process of correcting misfits, while only the variety in the misfits, which must be corrected, is relevant. Commonly, this variety is smaller than would be implied by the size of the system because of the presence of constraints (Ashby 1963, 244). The concept of constraints represents a contrasting view on complexity and its implications for adaptation, which speaks directly to the research questions raised by the Burton et al. (2002) study. Next, we will introduce the concept in more detail.

Ashby (1963, 127) offers an example of what is meant by constraints: The observable colors of traffic lights are red, yellow, and green. Since many more colors exist than could be lit, a constraint exists. They are further constrained because the colors are only lit in certain time sequences: first red, then red and yellow, then green, etc. Thus only four combinations are used out of the possible eight so that another type of constraint exists.

Constraints are fundamental to design, and in this chapter, we will unfold the concept in more detail as we go along. First and foremost, however, the concept of constraint applies to both causes and effects. The effects are more manifest and easier to observe and study. Rain only comes from one direction rather than many so that the manifest effects from gravity are constraints on the direction from which rain comes. This simplifies the design of housing in general and the removal of misfits pertaining to rain in particular. Decision makers do not evaluate all possible alternatives, but only search in a more limited subset until a satisfactory solution presents itself. In the social sciences, manifest effects from bounded, or constrained, rationality cause a significant reduction in the number of solutions that a decision maker can or must consider in order to solve a problem. In Ashby's example of the traffic lights, the combination and sequence of colors in the traffic lights are the manifest effects from underlying causes, which in this case are subject to (technical) design. In a similar way, as organizations grow from small to large, misfits proceed in certain sequences that are not random.

Finally, for our discussions here, we will use the information processing (IP) view as an analytic framework. We do so because it is generally accepted as a valid framework, because it complies with the framework used by Burton et al. (2002), and, in particular, because it is built on the concepts of bounded rationality, which makes it particularly well suited for the analysis of constraints. In the IP view, the demand for IP must be met by the organizations capacity to process information in order to be in fit. A misfit is present if there is a difference between IP demand and capacity. There are two strategies for removing a misfit: reduce the demand or increase the capacity. The first strategy is particularly relevant for dealing with problems of complexity, as first pointed out by Ashby (1963), because overall IP capacity is limited or, as Arrow (1974) put it, there are limits to organization.

The overall IP capacity of the organization is determined by its repertoire of information processing components. Each component has its own capacity and costs, and they are added rather than substituted for others, although some substitution can take place (Galbraith 1977, 53–54; Klaas, Lauridsen, and Håkonsson 2006). For example, hierarchical information structure has a certain amount of IP capacity. If this is insufficient, rules can be developed that have their own IP capacity (in the sense that they provide information that is processed a priori, thus diminishing the load on the hierarchy accordingly so that the hierarchy can focus only on exceptions to the rules). The rules, and the IP capacity that they provide, are thus added to that of the hierarchy, and so overall IP capacity is increased to meet increases in demand. In this way, each organizational component has a certain IP capacity, and the overall IP capacity is a function of the individual IP capacity of its constituent components. In this perspective, multi-contingency fit implies that the IP demand that the organization faces must be somehow balanced with its IP capacity both on the overall organizational level as well as on the component level.

Hypothesis

For SARFIT to be valid in a multi-component framework, adaptation must be able to proceed in an incremental and continuous manner. This is only possible if misfits display constraints. Alternative theories claim, with reference to complexity, that adaptation is revolutionary and rare. As already discussed, there are two perspectives on complexity and constraints: the structural and the process perspective. In order to increase validity, we seek information in data from both perspectives, according to general principles of triangulation. We begin with the structural perspective and continue with process.

Structural Complexity versus Constraints

As mentioned, Ashby (1963) acknowledged that large systems are of particular interest, because they are complex and consist of many components. By "large" Ashby means that the number of components, N, tends to increase as the system grows in size, following the general notion that as the size of a system increases, it becomes more differentiated. This is true for biological, technical, and social systems; in social systems, the process of differentiation is driven by returns to scale in production and administration. Size refers to the number of employees—or members—in the organization (see Burton et al. 2002, 1471, on misfits related to organizational size).

If we apply the concept of constraints directly to the Burton et al. (2002) study and to the way we defined interdependency and complexity earlier, then the total number of observable misfit combinations is smaller than the number of components would imply. We can compare the total number of possible misfit combinations to a traffic light where all colors will light in different sequences. If constraints exist in the combination of misfits, it implies that only a limited subset of misfit combinations exist from the total number of possible combinations given the number of total misfits, N. Thus, if no constraints existed, then all 90 misfit combinations would commonly occur. In a system where misfits are linked together, the expectation is that the likelihood, or frequency, of the observed misfits is the same. In other words, in a population of organizations with misfits, the expectation is that all misfit types have the same probability of occurring. The expected distribution is the uniform, which reflects the completely unconstrained and random distribution.

But if constraints existed in Ashby's interpretation, then only a smaller subset of the 90 would manifest themselves while others would not so that the variety facing the designer would be much smaller than what would be implied by the size of the misfit system. Like the colors of the traffic light, some misfits will be much more common, while others are rare or even non-existent. This is reflected in the Pareto distribution when the misfit types are ranked in order of their frequency from high to low:

Hypothesis 1a: Complexity and interdependencies cause all 90 misfits to occur commonly. The distribution of misfit types is best described by a uniform distribution.

Hypothesis 1b: Constraints will cause some misfits to occur often and others seldom or never. The distribution of misfit types is best described by a Pareto distribution.

Hypothesis 1 focuses on constraints in terms of its effects. As mentioned earlier, the concept applies both to causes and effects. If Hypothesis 1a is to be true, then K must be large, and, more importantly, it must be constant. K is a measure of the number of other components that a component is linked to and must be aligned with. Kaufmann (1993) decided to model K as a constant so that for a certain value of K, all components in the system will have the same number of links to other components. There is what McKelvey (1999) termed homogeneity among components. As a consequence, each misfit will have the same frequency or likelihood of occurring. If, on the other hand, K may be subject to variation, then misfits will be clustered, or centralized, around components with many links, or a large K, while they will less frequently involve components with few links, or a low K. In this situation, we have heterogeneity among components (McKelvey 1999). Based on the two situations of homogeneity or heterogeneity among components, we may build a second hypothesis for inquiring into the cause of the observed manifest effects of complexity and constraints:

Hypothesis 2a: K is constant, reflecting homogeneity among components.

Hypothesis 2b: K is subject to variation, reflecting heterogeneity among components.

Next, we turn to the adaptation process.

The Adaptation Process and Performance Effects from Misfit Reduction

In the SARFIT model, the incentive to adapt the organization by removing misfits is the increase in performance. Earlier, we explained how the SARFIT model will also work in a multi-misfit context under the assumption that constraints exist, thus reducing the variety in misfits. But if constraints do not exist, then the entire system becomes very complex and SARFIT will not work; on the contrary, rather than improving performance by removing misfits, it may create more misfits and deteriorate performance further (Burton et al. 2002).

Depending on whether misfits are constrained or complex, different distributions of the number of, or frequency of, misfits in organizations are expected. These distributions, we argue, reflect differences in the adaptation process. If adaptation is continuous, based on a process of ongoing performance improvements driven by sequential removals of misfits as SARFIT holds, then most organizations would have a limited number of misfits, while very few would have none and very few very many; in other words, for continuous adaptation, we would expect that the number of misfits in a population of organizations would be normally distributed because most of the organizations would be in a continual and incremental process of change and adaptation.

On the other hand, if removing misfits is complex and uncertain and only a lack of any misfits leads to significantly better performance (Burton et al. 2002, 1480), we expect a u-shaped, bimodal distribution. Because there is a strong incentive to stay with a certain configuration, even if environments have changed, change is rare, revolutionary, and uncertain (Hannan and Freeman 1984; Levinthal 1997; Miller and Friesen 1980; Rivkin 2000; Sastry 1997; Tushman and Romanelli 1985). This implies that many organizations in a sample would have no misfits. But for those who eventually change, the changes are revolutionary, so many misfits, simultaneously involving many or all of the components of the organization, are evident. This leads to the expectation that a smaller number of organizations will hold most of the misfits in the sample, while most would have none, or, at least, those organizations that are in misfit all have many misfits since change is revolutionary:

> *Hypothesis 3a*: Due to complexity, adaptation and change is rare and revolutionary. Misfits in a population of organizations follow a bimodal distribution, with many organizations having no misfits and a smaller number of organizations having many misfits.
> *Hypothesis 3b*: Due to constraints, adaptation and change is continuous and sequential. Misfits in a population of organizations follow a normal distribution, with many organizations having some misfits and few having none or many misfits.

A second aspect of the adaptation process is related more directly to the concepts of interdependency and complexity. Earlier we explained the concepts of interdependency and complexity of a system with N components and K links. We also referred to the Burton et al. application of these concepts in a system with $N = 90$ misfits and with K links between them.

When a misfit emerges, e.g., from organizational growth (see Donaldson's discussion of how misfits emerge, 2001, 247), removing the misfit may or may not create new misfits, depending on whether the misfit is linked to other misfits, or not. When $K = 0$, the misfit can be removed by adjusting the value, or state, in one of the two components that must be realigned to achieve fit without creating any new misfits or effecting the performance contribution of any other components. When $K = 3$, then three new misfits, and with them diminished performance, will be created. Therefore, in this situation, the designer must simultaneously consider and remove all four misfits in order to improve performance. The complexity of this task may still be manageable and continuous adaptation according to SARFIT still feasible. But if K is larger, then removing the first misfit will create an overwhelmingly large number of new misfits accompanied by significant loss of performance because the entire configuration gets misaligned. Like the other questions we have raised in this chapter, whether removing a misfit through the process of adjusting the value, or state, of a component in order to achieve realignment with another will create more misfits or not is ultimately an empirical question:

> *Hypothesis 4a*: Due to high levels of interdependency and complexity, removing misfits one at a time will create more misfits.
> *Hypothesis 4b*: Due to constraints, removing misfits one at a time will create fewer misfits.

Analysis and Results

Data used for the study was the SME database, supplied with financial data for 1996–97, which was also used by the Burton et al. (2002) study; see their study for details. All calculations were done using the SAS Version 9.4 for Windows X64 software.

For each proposition regarding misfit, a binary indicator was constructed, assuming the value 1 if the company was found to misfit on the statement and 0 otherwise. Thus, for example, ES1 = 1 if the company operated in a low uncertainty environment and had a prospector strategy, and ES1 = 0 otherwise. For a complete overview of the statements, please refer to the Burton et al. (2002) study. It is noticed that the statement C5 was not defined, as machine bureaucracy was not included in the data.

To test Hypothesis 1, we calculated for each firm the number of misfit statements that the firm misfitted on as well as the sum of these. These figures varied from 0 to 18 misfits in all. Figure 2.1 (p. 26) provides a histogram for the number of misfits.

The summary statistics behind this distribution are mean = 17.84, standard deviation = 27.20, standard error for the mean = 2.90, 95% confidence interval for the mean = [12.16; 23.52] and median = 7, which is far below the value of the mean and below its confidence interval. The 25% and 75% quartiles are 2 and 24, respectively, which is far from symmetrical around the mean. The skewness coefficient = 2.92, and the kurtosis coefficient = 9.70. Both are thus significantly above zero, thus indicating a right skewed and widespread distribution. Thus, in conclusion, a Pareto distribution, and not a normal distribution, is a valid description of the misfit data, reflecting a situation where some misfits are very common or frequent, while most are not. In summary, this supports Hypothesis 1b. If the distribution was uniform, reflecting Hypothesis 1a, then the expected frequency of each misfit would be 18. But the misfits that the designer is most likely to encounter are E8 "high centralization and highly turbulent environments"

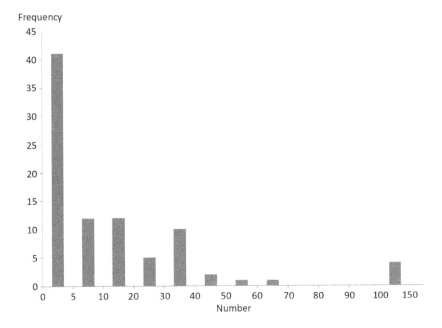

Figure 2.1 Frequency distribution of number of misfits

(frequency = 148 misfits), Si6 "small-sized organization and high organizational complexity" (132), and CE3 "developmental climate with low environmental equivocality" (102). As discussed previously, the distribution of the misfits are the manifest effects of underlying causes so that if the distribution is of a Pareto type, then we would expect to see variation in the value of K as the underlying cause. We expressed this in Hypothesis 2, which we turn to next.

Analyzing all 89 misfit statements reveals that K is neither high nor constant. The highest theoretical value that K could take in the sample is $(N - 1) = 88$; the highest actual value for K in the sample is eight (internal process climate), while the lowest is one (rational goal climate). In Table 2.1, we have listed some misfits that reflect differences in K. In the table, the first column is the misfit number, or code, as it appears in the Burton et al. (2002) study. In the next column it is stated which two components are in misfit. For example, for the first row, misfit E8 is between the two components environment and degree of centralization. If the environment is in a state of low equivocality, high complexity, and high uncertainty, then a high degree of centralization is a misfit. The two last columns—frequency of misfits— are discussed later in the chapter. From the table, we can see that there are eight misfit statements involving high centralization so that $K = 7$. Looking at the management climate component, we similarly get for internal process

Table 2.1 Frequencies of Some Existing and New Misfit Relationships

Misfit	Misfit relationship	Frequency of misfits	
		Existing	*New*
	High-centralization misfits		
E8	Low equivoc.—high complex—high uncert.—high central	148	
E16	High equivoc.—high complex—high uncert.—high central	34	
S4	Prospector—high central	37	
T7	Non-routine—high central	37	
Si4	Large size—high central	57	
C4	Group climate—high central	36	
C9	Developmental climate—high central	101	
M8	Low microinvolvement—high central	44	
	Total no. of existing misfits:	**494**	
	Low centralization misfits		
S8	Analyzer without innovation—low centralization	4	34
S12	Defender—low centralization	2	26
M4	High microinvolvement—low centralization	9	66
		15	126
	Total no. of new misfits:		**(126–15) = 111**
	High-organizational complexity misfits		
Si6	Small-size organization—high org. complexity	*132*	
	Low organizational complexity misfits		
S7	Analyzer without innovation—low org. complexity	1	34/20
S11	Defender—low org. complexity	1	26/17
T3	High routine—low org. complexity	2	74/27
C13	Internal process—low org. complexity	1	19/7
		5	153/71
	Total no. of new misfits:		**(71–5) = 66**
	Climate misfits (others than rational goal climate)		
CE1	Group—high equivocality	32	
CE2	Internal process—high equivocality	2	
CE3	Developmental—low equivocality	102	
CE4	Developmental—low uncertainty	17	
CS1	Internal process—analyzer with innovation	4	
CS2	Internal process—prospector	3	
CS3	Group—prospector	11	
CS4	Developmental—defender	16	

(*continued*)

Table 2.1 Continued

Misfit	Misfit relationship	Frequency of misfits	
		Existing	New
CT1	Internal process—non-routine	1	
CT2	Developmental—routine	47	
CM 1	Group—high microinvolvement	20	
CM2	Developmental—high microinvolvement	35	
CM3	Internal process—low microinvolvement	7	
C1	Group—functional configuration	30	
C2	Group—high formalization	7	
C3	Group—high-organizational complexity	18	
C4	Group—high centralization	36	
C6	Developmental—functional configuration	70	
C7	Developmental—high formalization	22	
C8	Developmental—high-organizational complexity	35	
C9	Developmental—high centralization	101	
C10	Internal process—simple configuration	4	
C11	Internal process—matrix configuration	4	
C12	Internal process—low formalization	2	
C13	Internal process—low organizational complexity	1	
	Total no. of existing misfits:	627	
	Rational goal climate misfits		
C14	Rational goal—high formalization	5	31
CM14	Rational goal—low microinvolvement	10	39
	Total no. of new misfits:		70

climate $K = 8$, for developmental climate $K = 7$, for group climate $K = 5$, and for rational goal climate $K = 1$.

Next, we looked at the distribution of misfits as it was stated in Hypothesis 3. This hypothesis focused on the expected adaptation process, which may be either rare or revolutionary because of complexity, or incremental and continuous with the presence of constraints. In Figure 2.2 (p. 29), the distribution of the number of misfits that the organization has in the Burton et al. (2002) study is shown.

The summary statistics behind this distribution are mean = 7.01, standard deviation = 3.47, standard error for the mean = 0.23, 95% confidence interval for the mean = [6.55; 7.47] median = 7, which is close to the value of the mean and inside its confidence interval. The 25% and 75% quartiles are 5 and 9, respectively, which is symmetrical around the mean. The

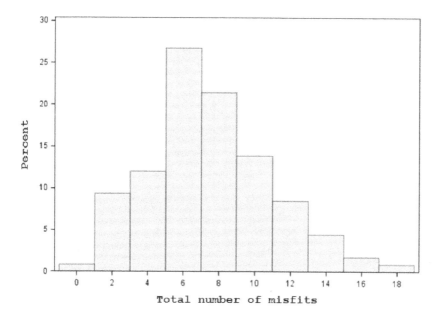

Figure 2.2 Frequency distribution of misfits in the organization

skewness coefficient = 0.51, and the kurtosis coefficient = 0.14. Both are thus very close to 0. Thus, in conclusion, a normal distribution with mean 7.01 and standard deviation of 3.47 is a valid description of the misfit data. This result supports Hypothesis 3b, which states that organizational adaptation, as SARFIT holds, is continuous and incremental rather than rare and revolutionary.

The last hypothesis looked at another aspect of the adaptation process and related directly to the conclusion of the Burton et al. (2002) study, suggesting that removing misfits may create more rather than fewer misfits. Thus, departing from Hypothesis 3, if adaptation is rare and revolutionary, we would expect to see more misfits created than removed while the opposite should be valid for adaptation to be continuous and incremental. We formulated this in Hypothesis 4.

In Figure 2.3 (p. 30), the cluster of misfits involving high centralization is shown. In the figure, each misfit is marked according to Burton et al. (2002); e.g., T7 is the misfit between high centralization and a non-routine technology. Each misfit relationship in the figure also displays two numbers: the first is the actual frequency of misfits found in the data, and the second is the expected frequency of misfits if all misfits would appear with the same (average) frequency in a uniform distribution. For example, the T7 high-centralization, non-routine misfit has an actual frequency of 37 and an expected frequency of 18. The expected average frequency of a misfit,

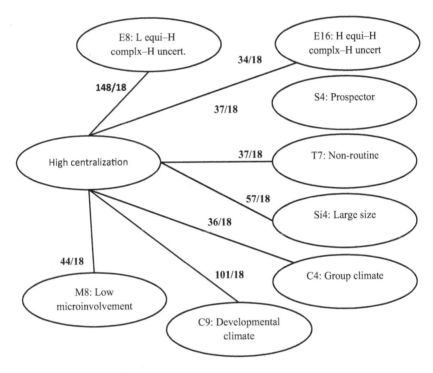

Figure 2.3 Misfits involving high centralization

assuming a uniform distribution, is the total number of misfits divided by the number of misfit types, i.e., (1,570/89) = 17.6, which is rounded off to 18.

Revisiting Table 2.1, the third and fourth columns relate to the frequency of misfits. Column 3 counts the number of existing misfits as they appear in the data of the Burton et al. study. Column 4 counts the number of new misfits that would be created in the sample, if the value, or state, of one component would be changed to a new one in order to remove misfits. For example, if the degree of centralization were changed from high to low, then 34 new misfits would be created for organizations with an analyzer without innovation strategy (misfit S8); for those companies with a defender strategy, it would be 26 (misfit S12), etc. From the figure, it is evident that by simply decreasing the level of centralization, the designer can remove a large number of misfits, totaling 494 misfits or ((494/1570)*100) = 31% of all misfits. This situation suggests that significant constraints exist; if there were no constraints at all, then each misfit relationship would occur with the same frequency, thus reducing the degree of centralization in the afore-mentioned structure in this case only to remove (8 x 18) = 144 misfits, or 9.1% of all misfits in the sample.

Revisiting Table 2.1, another frequent misfit was the Si6 "small-size and high-organizational complexity" misfit, which appeared 132 times. If organizational complexity is changed from high to low, potentially a total of 153 new misfits are created. However, reviewing the misfits involving low complexity, several—such as high routine—misfits seems to pertain to larger organizations. Controlling for size in the new misfits might be expected to reduce the number of misfits related to the small organizations. Therefore, the number of new misfits for small organizations is also shown in the table, so; e.g., the T3 "high-routine and low-complexity" misfit would only apply to 27 small firms. This is indicated in the fourth column as the number behind the slash. Thus when controlling for small size, changing organizational complexity from high to low would fix 132 misfits while creating 66 new ones.

A third interesting result emerged when analyzing the misfits related to managerial climate. According to Table 2.1, in all, 27 misfit types are related to the managerial climate, with a total of 627 misfits in the sample. Of the 27 different misfit types, 9 involved a process climate, 8 a developmental climate, and 6 a group climate, while 2 were related to a rational goal climate. Thus the value of K for the management climate component is variable and dependent on its value, or state. If the state of the management climate component is changed from a high to a low K state, then a larger number of existing misfits will be removed while fewer new ones will be created. Thus, referring to the table, there are only 15 existing misfits related to the rational goal climate, compared to a total of 627 existing misfits for the 3 other climate types; if the climate was changed to a rational goal climate in all companies in the sample, then 627 existing misfits would be removed and 70 new ones created.

If we combine removing the high-centralization misfits, high-organizational complexity misfits, and the climate misfits and take into account that two of the climate misfits—C4 and C9—are also counted in the high-centralization misfits, then changing the value of only three components (centralization, organizational complexity and managerial climate) will remove (494 + 132 + 627 − 36 − 101) = 1,116 misfits out of a total of 1,570 misfits in the sample. At the same time (111 + 66 + 70) = 247 new misfits will be created so that more existing misfits are removed than new ones created. Overall, (869/1570 x 100) % = 55% of all misfits in the sample may be removed by changing the state of three components so that there is strong support for Hypothesis 4b, which hypothesized that more misfits will be removed than new ones created when using an incremental approach to removing misfits.

Discussion

Overall, the results from our analysis indicate that continuous change and adaptation by an incremental process of misfit removal can work surprisingly well. Our study reveals that the way misfits are structured reflects significant constraints, providing information for the designer from which to economize on when designing appropriate information processing structures. There are several important implications from our results. The most important one is the implication for the dynamic aspects of organizational structure and design. For instance, managerial climate has been established as a contingency, and so Burton and Obel (2004, 146) identify four climate types that each represent four different ways of processing information. They proceed to identify how each way of information processing represents the most effective and/or efficient fit with structure. If the structure needs to be changed, information processing is changed and a misfit will emerge with the current climate. The climate must also be changed to remove the misfit and create new alignment between the information processing capacity and demand of structure and climate. However, our analysis of the misfit structure revealed that there are significant differences in climates in terms of their dynamic properties. Three of the climates are very susceptible to change in other components, while the fourth—rational goal climate—is not. For the rational goal climate, changes in most other components, except for two, will not require a change in the rational goal climate. For the three other climates, the probability that they will need to change as a consequence of changes in other structural components is much higher, and, accordingly, our study also finds that the number of misfits related to them is much more frequent.

The misfit analysis of climate illustrates how the static properties of the structure-contingency alignment may be different from the dynamic. If we assume that organizations need to change on an ongoing basis, then—and this is the point—some components, which may represent a good solution to achieve static fit, will represent a poor solution to achieve fit over time, as the organization needs to change its overall design or information processing capacity to realign with changes in the demand. Dynamic fit is the alignment of IP demand and IP capacity over time. The concept is different from static fit because it involves time and costs of change as parameters (Klaas 2004, 2010, 2013). Previous studies of climate as a contingency has shown how all four climate types may represent static fit or misfit with structural components. A major contribution from our study is the finding that the dynamic properties of the rational goal climate are much better—in terms of dynamic fit—than the three others, or, more generally, that the study of the dynamic properties of components may lead to modified—and better—design solutions than the ones derived from only static, comparative studies.

Our findings on different static and dynamic properties add empirical evidence to recent theoretical findings. The static and dynamic properties may also be evaluated in terms of content and process costs (Barnett and Carroll 1995). Content costs are the costs related to lack of change, or misfit; process costs are the costs related to change, or removing misfits. Relating these two types of costs to Hypothesis 3, a low/high ratio of content to process costs would lead to the expectation that change is rare and revolutionary; if the ratio of content costs is high relative to process costs, this would favor continuous and incremental change. Our findings about the dynamic properties of managerial climate lends empirical support to the hypothesis that process costs may be much lower than assumed so far and why this is so. Håkonsson, Klaas, and Carroll (2013), in a theoretical study using computational modeling, reached a similar conclusion. Process costs are related to the loss of competency, which follows change so that inertia preserves the competency base of the company. With revolutionary change, a large loss of inertia and competency causes very poor organizational performance and reliability. Their study showed how large losses of competency could be avoided by increasing the organization's capacity to build new competencies, leading to lower process costs. The lower process costs lead to more ongoing change, which in turn caused lower content costs; as a result, with continuous adaptation, the organization performed better and more reliably than with rare and revolutionary change. Our empirical results in this chapter yield additional insights into how process costs may be lowered by means of the right organizational design. Design components have a variable number of causal links, K, depending on their state; identifying and using components with few links will reduce process costs, because fewer links between components will cause fewer components into the need of changing states, as the organization is continuously adapted to changes in its environment. More research into and better understanding of the dynamic properties of organization design components should enable lower process costs and more reliable change and adaptation to take place.

Our study also offers insights into the nature of the observed constraints and how they may be levered by the designer. Thus we were able to identify several aspects, or principles, of how structural constraints may be utilized by the designer. First, some misfit types are much more frequent than others. We found that this is related to the presence of misfits clustered around specific components with a high K; i.e., it is connected to many other components, which themselves are less connected, or with lower K. This was the case with high-centralization and high-organizational complexity, involving 31% and 8% of all misfits, respectively. Of the 224 firms in the sample, 148 had misfit on high centralization. The presence of such critical misfits allow the designer to focus on a very small subset of components, such as centralization or organizational complexity, and remove a disproportionately large number of misfits by changing the state of the critical component so that its new state represents a fit with the state of the many other components that it is linked to. Klaas et al. (2006, 152) previously suggested that critical misfits exist and that a prioritized approach to fixing misfits is promising; our findings here adds empirical substance to the concept of critical misfits.

The removal of critical misfits is based on exploiting heterogeneity in the number of causal links, K, between the components, by focusing on the components with many links rather than the ones with few. Appropriately changing the state of high K components will realign them with many other components and remove many misfits. Here heterogeneity refers to the variation in K across different components. Another strategy for economizing on misfits is to focus on variation in K between different states of the same component, as in the case of climate just discussed. Here removing misfits is not based on realignment but on disconnection—removing causal links by changing the state of the component from one with a high K to one with a low K. This novel finding adds empirical insights into how decomposition of the overall complex system into more manageable subsystems may be achieved in the design of organizations. A nearly decomposable (ND) system is one that maximizes the interaction within its subsystems and minimizes them between (Foss 2008; Simon 2002), or, in the terms used here, K is high within a subsystem and low between them. Our finding illustrates the critical role that assumptions—implicit or explicit—about homogeneity and/or heterogeneity between components play when using the N,K model as analytical framework. Studies using the Kaufmann (1993) model—most of them computational—implicitly accepted his assumption of homogeneity, and so the focus in the discourse has been on complexity as a function of the number of links between components, K. But as our study discloses, there is no empirical basis for this assumption in organization design, and, furthermore, the implications from variation in the number K is more important for the study of complexity than is the number itself. McKelvey (1999) aptly made this point, which made Anderson, Meyer, Eisenhardt, Carley, and Pettigrew (1999, 234) conclude that his analysis should be "required reading for scholars interested in this particular approach." Analytically, the concept of constraints, as we have discussed it here, is synonymous with assuming heterogeneity. If there is no variation in the value of K, then it is decided a priori that no constraints can exist. Computational models demonstrate the immutable logical consequences of a set of premises. Pertaining to the computational studies of complexity in organization theory and design (Levinthal 1997; Rivkin 2000), our empirical findings question the premise of holding K constant in these models and, as a result, the conclusions derived from them about complexity causing adaptation to be of a random, uncertain, and revolutionary nature.

The concept of constraints holds the key to unfolding decomposition and the application of ND structures because it is subject to direct empirical investigation. A better and more detailed understanding of the nature of constraints offers a significant opportunity to learn more about effective and efficient organization design in a static as well as in a dynamic perspective. Our present study highlighted centralization as an important source of constraints. In previous studies, organizational size has been identified as another source for constraints. In a computational study using the information processing framework, Klaas (2010) found that organizational size and information architecture varied systematically with structural and environmental constraints. Because of bounded rationality, the overall information capacity of the structure is limited. The design problem is to create an architecture that balances the capacity of information processing with its demand. IP demand origins internally and externally: externally from the rate of change in the environment and internally from the coordination load that increases with size, specialization, and technology.

Large organizations meet high internal demands for information processing caused by specialization: the more specialization, the more coordination is needed. Because overall IP capacity is constrained due to bounded rationality, increase in external demand for IP has to be set off by reduction in internal demand by means of reducing size and the degree of specialization. In a preliminary empirical test, Klaas and Lauridsen (2010) were able to validate size as a manifest constraint. Using the same dataset as the one analyzed in this chapter, they found that size varied with environmental rate of change as predicted by the computational study. They found a very strong negative correlation between size, measured as number of employees and environmental change rate. They also found a significant negative correlation between technology, measured as coordination intensiveness and environmental change rate. In a two-by-two matrix plot of size and environmental change, most observations were seen in the small-size/low-change rate quadrant, some in the small-size/high-change and large-size/low-change quadrants but none in the large-size/high-change quadrant. This distribution is what was predicted by the computational study of information processing (Klaas 2010, 378). Similarly to the example of traffic lights, constraints rule out a number of misfits, such as misfits related to combinations of large-size, high-environmental change rate and coordination-intensive technologies.

In a dynamic context, time acts as an important constraint on a very fundamental level, to the extent that the second law of thermodynamics applies to social organization. The idea behind this dynamic physical law is reflected in the statement, "You cannot un-fry a fried egg." In Ashby's example of the traffic light, the chronological sequence of the three colors constraints the number of color combinations from eight to four. In the same manner, misfits are often tied to a particular developmental phase in the organizations life; indeed, as Greiner pointed out, misfits are often related to transitions from one phase to the next. Most, if not all, types of misfits are constrained to a particular transitional phase; knowledge about which types of misfits are related to each transitional phase greatly reduces the complexity of the design problem so that the process of removing misfits is not random but selective. Burton and Obel (2004, 388), under the heading of lifecycle management, point out that change is not random and offer an overview of the specific component states, or values, for each phase. Chronological developments in organization design is another reason why a better understanding of the dynamics of organization design in general, and temporal constraints in particular, has potential for modifying and improving design solutions originally developed from static fit.

Size and degree of differentiation is often a manifestation of time, as most organizations grow from being small and undifferentiated to becoming larger and more differentiated over time. Thus temporal constraints again points back to the critical role that organizational size has. Donaldson and Joffe (2014) discuss size as one of the three most important contingencies which the manager must take into account. As size increases, the hierarchy increases but at a lower rate, so the relative costs of hierarchy decrease with size. Burton and Obel (2004), in their multi-contingency model, have size as one in a total of six strategic contingencies. They note that size is a special contingency because it not only defines the demand for IP but also the capacity. The problem is rooted in the fundamental tension between specialization and coordination; to overcome limitations in the individual's rationality, organizations specialize in information processing so that capacity for IP is increased with size; however, information has to be coordinated to be of any use for the organization, and so coordination, and with this IP demand, increases as size increases (Arrow 1974). Thus, for size, an imperative view as it is discussed in Luo et al.'s chapter in his anthology is too simplistic. As we have seen, size is the source of many important constraints that the designer may exploit. For example, constraints in individual and organization IP capacity and the trade-offs between the IP demand from internal coordination, technology, and the external environment, as well as the temporal constraints that may be embedded within the organization's current development phase as it is reflected in its current size and degree of differentiation. This allows the designer to understand which misfits to disregard, as they belong to past developments, and which to expect and look for in the future.

An important point from the managerial perspective is that constraints may not just emerge from physical laws and other law-like constraints, such as bounded rationality; they may also be created by the designer. A classic example of managerially established constraints is that of ambidexterity or, in broader terms, structural separation. Binns and Tushman as well as Luo et al. in their chapters in the present volume discuss the pros and cons of this approach to constraints. The ultimate separation is the spin-off or the division of one business into two separate business firms, which is a frequent and often successful approach to the problems associated with a complex misfit situation; the separation introduces constraints in the misfits of each new separate unit, simplifying and thus reducing both content and process costs compared to the unconstrained situation. Another classic managerial approach is to introduce temporal constraints as we already discussed them. In their seminal papers, Brown and Eisenhardt (1997) and Eisenhardt and Brown (1998) showed how the introduction of temporal constraints in terms of "time pacing" allowed companies to adapt to a fast-changing environment on a continuous basis. This direct link between temporal constraints and continuous adaptation was also found in the Håkonsson et al.'s (2013, 188) study of the structural properties of continuous change. They found that creating a dynamic-fit routine, in which adaptation was not reactive and driven by poor performance but was proactive, was a prerequisite for changing the adaptive behavior of an inertia-generating system from revolutionary to continuous change mode.

Business re-engineering, divesting, and focusing on core business are yet another way of introducing constraints to a misfit situation that is becoming too complex. The Confederation of Danish Industry has recently developed a methodology called "simplimize" (www.simplimize.dk; in Danish only), in which the complexity of the company's product portfolio is reduced significantly. The constraint causes a reduction in IP demand and illustrates, with the other examples, a fundamental and general principle of removing misfits by reducing the demand for IP by means of constraints as an alternative to increasing structural IP capacity. Ashby's Law of Requisite Variety states that only variety can destroy variety. This law is reflected in the IP views definition of fit as IP demand has to be met with IP capacity. As Ashby (1963, 245) points out, the law places an absolute limit to the amount of regulation that can happen if IP capacity is limited and that constraints, by the law of requisite variety, means that complexity is less than what otherwise would be the case. If the capacity to deal with complexity in misfits is limited, then the discovery of a constraint is the only way the designer can find a solution to the design problem and restore fit (Ashby 1963, 247). So the implications from the law of requisite variety on multi-contingency frameworks are not only that variety must be matched by variety, but more specifically that variety has to be somehow reduced and that constraints are the only way of doing so. With a complex misfit situation, the attempt to remove the misfits by making appropriate changes in the state of many components is futile. The designer must first look for, and introduce, proper constraints that will remove misfits without having to change the state of the corresponding components.

Conclusion

Donaldson's (1987, 1999) Structural Adaptation to Regain Fit (SARFIT) model explains how structural adaptation is driven by decrease in performance, or fitness, from misfits. SARFIT represents a single-contingency, single-misfit framework. But organizations are differentiated and complex systems include multiple contingencies and misfits. Is SARFIT also valid in this context?

In this chapter, we did an empirical investigation of complexity and constraints in a multi-contingency framework with multiple misfits. Complexity may lead to a situation where functionalist adaptation may not work and change becomes rare, revolutionary, and risky. On the other hand, constraints may lead to a situation where functionalist adaptation works well and change is continuous, incremental, and reliable.

We revisited the Burton et al. (2002) dataset with 89 different misfit types in a population of 224 firms with a total of 1,570 misfits. The results suggest that significant constraints reduce the potential complexity of the many misfits and that an incremental approach to fixing misfits, according to SARFIT, works surprisingly well. We also found empirical support for adaptation as a process of continuous and incremental removal of misfits while we found no support for rare and revolutionary adaptation. Our results support a small but growing body of research that investigates how complex organizations with inertia do not necessarily adapt in revolutionary and risky ways, but engage in reliable and continuous adaptation and change.

A novel finding is that design components can have differential static and dynamic properties. This has significant impact on the process costs related to adaptation and is caused by differences in interdependency depending on which state the component is in. If interdependency is high, then the component is much more prone to needing change when adjustments are made in other parts of the organization, and vice versa. Identifying and utilizing components with good dynamic properties in terms of low-process costs is critical for achieving dynamic fit and represents an important area for further research.

Another important result is the critical role that constraints play when facing complexity. Introducing a constraint will reduce the demand for information processing, and this may in many cases be the only viable way of balancing IP demand with capacity and to regain fit. We presented a number of different constraints that the designer can take advantage of; however, more research is needed to unfold the full potential of this approach to regaining fit. It was also highlighted that SARFIT and the contingency imperative needs further development. First, the aggregation of individual, bivariate misfits into multi-contingency models has not yet reached a state where they are validated empirically. Thus more theoretical work has to be done in this area, followed by further tests. Second, the contingency imperative in its current interpretation is too mechanistic. As it stands, the contingency specifies the level of information processing demand that the structure must meet with a corresponding capacity. But IP capacity is limited, and so often the only way to regain fit is by reducing the demand for IP. This requires that (some) contingencies are subject to managerial control, which is the case, e.g., with strategy and technology. In reducing the level of the contingency, the demand for IP does not violate the basic assumptions of SARFIT. As we discussed here, this follows directly from the more fundamental theories on which SARFIT is founded.

***

To Lex Donaldson, teacher and friend.

***

References

Alexander, C. 1964. *Notes on the synthesis of form.* Cambridge, MA: Harvard University Press.

Anderson, P., A. Meyer, K. Eisenhardt, K. Carley, and A. Pettigrew. 1999. Introduction to the special issue: Applications of complexity theory to organization science. *Organization Science* 10 (3):233–36.

Arrow, K. 1974. *The limits of organization.* New York: W. W. Norton.

Ashby, W. R. 1963. *An introduction to cybernetics.* 2nd ed. New York: Wiley.

Barnett, W. P. and G. R. Carroll. 1995. Modelling internal organizational change. *Annual Review of Sociology* 21:217–36.

Brown, S. L. and K. M. Eisenhardt. 1997. The art of continuous change: Linking complexity theory and time-paced evolution in relentlessly shifting organizations. *Administrative Science Quarterly* 42:1–34.Burton, R. M., J. T. Lauridsen, and B. Obel. 2002. Return on assets loss from situational and contingency misfits. *Management Science* 48 (11):1461–85.

Burton, R. M. and B. Obel. 2004. *Strategic organizational design.* Boston: Kluwer.

Caspin-Wagner, K., A. Y. Lewin, S. Massini, and C. Peeters. 2013. The underexplored role of managing interdependence fit in organization design and performance. *Journal of Organization Design* 2 (1):3–41.

Donaldson, L. 1987. Strategy and structural adjustment to regain fit and performance: In defense of contingency theory. *Journal of Management Studies* 24 (1):1–34.

Donaldson, L. 1996. The normal science of structural contingency theory. In *Handbook of organization studies.* Clegg, S., C. Hardy, and W. R. Nord, eds. London: Sage.

Donaldson, L. 1999. *Performance driven organizational change.* Thousand Oaks, CA: Sage.

Donaldson, L. 2001. *The contingency theory of organizations.* Thousand Oaks, CA: Sage.

Donaldson, L. and G. Joffe. 2014. Fit—The key to organizational design. *Journal of Organization Design* 3 (3):38–45.

Eisenhardt, K. M. and S. L. Brown. 1998. Time pacing: Competing in markets that won't stand still. *Harvard Business Review* 76 (2):59–70.

Foss, K. 2008. Will modular products and organizations improve lead-time in product development? In *Designing organizations: 21st century approaches.* Burton, R. M., B. H. Eriksen, D. D. Håkonsson, T. Knudsen, and C. C. Snow, eds. New York: Springer.Galbraith, J. R. 1977. *Organization design.* Reading, MA: Addison-Wesley.

Håkonsson, D. D., P. Klaas, and T. Carroll. 2013. The structural properties of sustainable, continuous change: Achieving reliability through flexibility. *Journal of Applied Behavioral Science* 49:179–205.

Hannan, M. T. and J. Freeman. 1984. Structural inertia and organizational change. *American Sociological Review* 49 (April):149–64.

Kaufmann, S. A. 1993. *The origins of order.* New York: Oxford University Press.

Klaas, P. 2004. *Towards a concept of dynamic fit in contingency theory.* Paper presented at the annual Systems Dynamic conference, Oxford, UK.

Klaas, P. 2010. *Insights into the dynamics of the open rational system.* Odense: University Press of Southern Denmark.

Klaas, P. 2013. *A conceptual model of dynamic fit and some implications for organizational structure.* Paper presented at ICOA workshop, University of Aarhus.

Klaas, P. and J. T. Lauridsen. 2010. *Scaling effects in misfit models: The iron law of size.* Paper presented at the 4th International Workshop on Organizational Design, Aarhus School of Business.

Klaas, P., J. T. Lauridsen, and D. D. Håkonsson. 2006. New developments in contingency fit theory. In *Designing organizations: 21st century approaches.* Burton, R. M., B. H. Eriksen, D. D. Håkonsson, T. Knudsen, and C. C. Snow, eds. New York: Springer.

Levinthal, D. A. 1997. Adaptation on rugged landscapes. *Management Science* 43 (7): 934–50.

March, J. G. and H. A. Simon. 1958. *Organizations*. New York: Wiley.

McKelvey, B. 1999. Avoiding complexity catastrophe in coevolutionary pockets: Strategies for rugged landscapes. *Organization Science* 10 (3):294–321.

Meyer, A. D., A. S. Tsui, and C. R. Hinings. 1993. Configurational approaches to organizational analysis. *Academy of Management Journal* 36 (3):1175–95.

Miller, D. and P. H. Friesen. 1980. Momentum and revolution in organizational adaptation. *Academy of Management Journal* 25:591–614.

Rivkin, J. W. 2000. Imitation on complex strategies. *Management Science* 46:824–44.

Sastry, M. A. 1997. Problems and paradoxes in a model of punctuated organizational change. *Administrative Science Quarterly* 42:237–75.

Simon, H. A. 1962. The architecture of complexity. *Proceedings of the American Philosophical Society* 106:67–82.

Simon, H. A. 2002. Near decomposability and the speed of evolution. *Industrial and Corporate Change* 11 (3):587–99.

Tushman, M. L. and E. Romanelli. 1985. Organizational evolution: A metamorphosis model of convergence and reorientation. *Research in Organizational Behavior* 7:171–222.

3 Fit of Structure to Multiple Contingencies

Equifinality versus the Contingency Imperative

Ben Nanfeng Luo, Lex Donaldson, and Kangkang Yu[1]

Introduction

Structural contingency theory is one established approach to organizational design. It holds that, in order to produce high performance, the structure of an organization needs to fit the contingencies of the organization (Burns and Stalker 1961; Burton, Lauridsen, and Obel 2002, 2003; Donaldson 2001; Van de Ven, Ganco, and Hinings 2013). More precisely, for high performance, the level of the structural variables, such as formalization, centralization, and specialization needs to fit the level required by the contingency variable. There is a contingency imperative: the contingency determines the structure that is required for the organization to avoid loss of performance, so the organization tends to adopt that structure (Donaldson 1982).

The early structural contingency literature focused on the fit of structure to a single contingency variable (e.g., Hage 1965; Thompson 1967). However, there can be more than one contingency variable for a structural variable (e.g., Burton et al. 2002, 2003; Child 1975; Donaldson 2001). It has been argued that when multiple contingencies exist simultaneously, they can produce a range of fitting structural levels, which all lead to the same high performance (Gresov 1989). This is referred to as equifinality—meaning that the same outcome can be attained from multiple initial states through multiple means (von Bertalanffy 1968). The contingency idea of a fit of structure to its contingencies is in the tradition of structural contingency theory. However, the equifinality idea of there being a range of organizational structures that fit a combination of multiple contingencies implies that managers can enjoy a wide choice of structures and thereby have strategic choice. Hence there is no contingency imperative.

It is vital to clarify whether equifinality or the contingency imperative is theoretically sounder, as these two perspectives provide conflicting design prescriptions. Equifinality suggests that organizational designers are less constrained by the contingencies and thus can enjoy free choice among *a set of* fitting structures. In contrast, the contingency imperative suggests that there is *only one single* level of the structure that fits these contingencies and thus organizational designers should try to adjust structure to this fitting level. If the contingency imperative is correct (i.e., only one single-fitting structure exists in the context of multiple contingencies), then most of the "fitting" structures proposed by the equifinality idea will actually be in misfit. If managers believe in equifinality, then, if they are in an organization with a misfitting structure, they may view it to be a fit and so may not see the need to adjust the organization's structure. In that situation, equifinality could be misleading and cause the organization to suffer performance loss.

This chapter examines the idea of fit to multiple contingencies and argues that equifinality and thus strategic choice may be uncommon and that there will usually be a contingency imperative in organizational design. The contributions of this chapter are threefold.

The first contribution is that it develops a conceptual framework to examine the contingency imperative versus equifinality debate in the context of organizational structure fitting multiple contingencies. This chapter integrates the literature of contingency theory, equifinality, and structural separation. It shows that three factors play roles in determining whether the contingency imperative or equifinality is theoretically sounder: the consistency of the requirements of multiple contingencies, the relative importance of these contingencies, and the availability of structural separation. This framework provides a roadmap for assessing the fits in the context of multiple contingencies.

The second contribution of this chapter is that it critically examines and redefines the concept of the *importance* of contingencies and shows that this is essential in order to distinguish where equifinality, rather than the contingency imperative, will apply. This chapter underscores that the importance of a contingency should be evaluated by the extent of performance loss resulting from each unit of deviation of the structure from the ideal structure prescribed by this contingency.

The third contribution is that it incorporates the concept of structural separation, including the organizational ambidexterity idea, reinterpreting it in terms of structural contingency fit, and showing that structural separation supports the contingency-imperative perspective. On those rare occasions when the condition for equifinality is met, structural separation means that, nevertheless, equifinality is avoided. Thus the chapter concludes that equifinality will be an even rarer event in organizational design, which, rather, is overwhelmingly subject to the contingency imperative.

In this chapter, through presenting the two approaches of the fit of structure to multiple contingencies, we attempt to shed light on the dispute between the contingency imperative and equifinality views. We will first discuss the structural contingency approach, demonstrating how the different combinations of two dimensions—the degree of conflict in the required structure and the importance of contingencies—lead to different theoretical conclusions. Then we will present the structural separation approach to show how conflicting requirements from multiple contingencies can be satisfied by the internal differentiation-and-integration pattern. A discussion of the implications is offered in the last section.

The Contingency Imperative and Equifinality in Contingency Theory

It has long been recognized that there is no universal way to design a structure, and in order to gain high performance, organizational structure needs to fit its contingencies (e.g., Burns and Stalker 1961; Donaldson 1987; Hage 1965; Lawrence and Lorsch 1967; Perrow 1967; Thompson 1967; Woodward 1965). This contingency perspective is still widely held in the organizational design literature (e.g., see chapters 1, 2, 4, and 6 in this volume; Birkinshaw, Nobel, and Ridderstrale 2002; Burton, Obel, and Håkonsson 2016; Carroll, Gormley, Bilardo, Burton and Woodman 2006; Egelhoff and Wolf 2016; Hollenbeck, Moon, Ellis, West, Ilgen, Sheppard, Porter, and Wagner III 2002; Klaas and Lauridsen 2016; Klaas, Lauridsen and Håkonsson 2006; Van de Ven, Leung, Bechara, and Sun 2012; Volberda, van der Weerdt, Verwaal, Stienstra, and Verdu 2012; Wasserman 2008). The term structure, in this chapter, is defined in a general sense. It subsumes major structural factors such as formalization, centralization, specialization (Pugh, Hickson, Hinings, and Turner 1968), and divisionalization (Rumelt 1974). Moreover, the contingency is defined as the situational factor with which the structural element needs to be aligned to avoid loss of organizational performance (Donaldson 2001). For instance, divisionalization fits a diversification strategy—that is, as the firm's products become diversified, its structure needs to move from being functional to being divisional (Chandler 1962). In this example, divisionalization is the structural variable, and diversification strategy is its contingency.

Some structural factors have only one contingency, which the structural factor needs to fit in order to produce high performance. However, some other structural factors each have two or more contingencies (Burton, Desanctis, and Obel 2006; Burton and Obel 1998; Burton et al. 2002, 2003; Child 1977, 1984; Donaldson 1985, 2001; Gresov 1989; Gresov and Drazin 1997; Klaas and Lauridsen 2016; Miller 1992; Mintzberg 1979; Sinha and Van de Ven 2005; Van de Ven and Drazin 1985). For instance, organizational formalization—defined as the extent to which the rules and standard operating procedures are introduced and exercised—needs to fit both environmental uncertainty (Burns and Stalker 1961; Lawrence and Lorsch 1967) and organizational size (Child 1975). The structure that has to fit more than one contingency is said to have "multiple contingencies" (Gresov 1989, 431).

The fact that organizations usually have multiple contingencies provides a more realistic picture of the complexity of organizational design (Drazin and Van de Ven 1985; Gresov 1990). However, this same fact also complicates the specification of the fitting structure, especially where the contingencies conflict. Multiple contingencies conflict with each other when they require different levels of the same structural variable (Child 1975; Gresov 1989; van Offenbeek, Sorge, and Knip 2009). This idea of conflicting contingencies is used to question the validity of structural contingency theory (Child 1977, 1984; Gresov and Drazin 1997). Some scholars argue that, whereas structural contingency theory is able to identify the fitting level of structure in single-contingency studies, it is not able to do so in situations with conflicting contingencies (e.g., Child 1977, 1984). This leads to a major qualification of the contingency fit idea in structural contingency theory.

When there are multiple contingencies, there can be two distinctive views about the number of fitting structures: the contingency-imperative and the equifinality views (Gresov 1989). The contingency imperative has the idea that the contingency determines the *fitting* structure, which produces high performance (Donaldson 1987). It emphasizes the specification of the fitting structure (Donaldson 1982). Accordingly, when there are multiple contingencies, the contingency-imperative idea holds that there is only one structure that will fit these multiple contingencies. In other words, to produce high performance, an organization needs to design a structure that is aligned with this ideal fitting structure.

On the other hand, equifinality is a concept that was articulated in biology by von Bertalanffy (1968), introduced to organization theory by Katz and Kahn (1966), and subsequently adopted by management scholars, including Doty, Glick, and Huber (1993), Jennings and Seaman (1994), Gresov and Drazin (1997), and Kang and Snell (2009). It is defined here as "the existence of several feasible equally effective design options for given contexts" (Van de Ven and Drazin 1985, 353). The equifinality view claims that there is more than one structure that is equally effective for the multiple contingencies. Thus organizational design can exercise strategic choice (Child 1972) between these equally effective structures.

After distinguishing the two distinctive views, the contingency imperative and equifinality, Gresov (1989) highlights that the relative importance of contingencies is pertinent to the discussion of conflicting contingencies. Specifically, when the contingencies are of unequal importance, there is only one ideal level of structure. In contrast, when the contingencies are equally important, there will be a range of equally effective designs. This focus on relative importance is a valuable insight by Gresov (1989). However, the criteria for establishing the importance of a contingency as proposed by Gresov (1989) are to some extent questionable, as will be shown in this chapter. Thus a new criterion is needed. This chapter argues for the need to refine Gresov's insight regarding the role of the relative importance of contingencies.

Moreover, the structural separation approach (Donaldson 2001; O'Reilly and Tushman 2004; Tushman and O'Reilly 1996), which emerged mostly from the literature on ambidexterity, can also shed light on the debate between the contingency imperative and equifinality views. We therefore bring structural separation into the discussion of the contingency imperative versus equifinality.

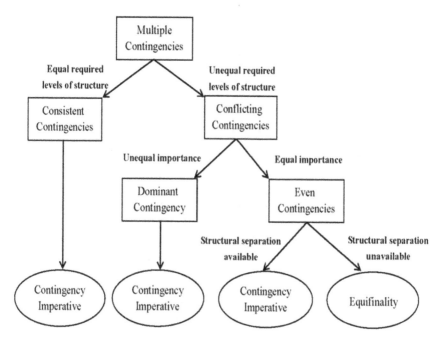

Figure 3.1 Summary of the main arguments

The main arguments of this chapter are laid out in Figure 3.1. The validity of equifinality versus the contingency imperative relies on three nested conditions: (1) the degree of conflict in the required structure, (2) the equality of the importance of contingencies to performance, and (3) the availability of a structural separation. Specifically, if two contingencies have equal required levels of structure, it is a consistent-contingencies circumstance, which leads to a contingency imperative. Conversely, if these two contingencies require unequal levels of structure to fit, it becomes a conflicting-contingencies situation. If these two conflicting contingencies have unequal importance for the performance of the organization, it is a dominant-contingency context, which supports a contingency imperative. In contrast, if the two conflicting contingencies have equal importance for the performance, they are even contingencies. Then, if structural separation is available, a contingency imperative is supported. Otherwise, equifinality is possible. These arguments will now be explained more fully.

The Structural Contingency Approach

In many structural contingency studies, the fit between structure and contingency is operationalized in a bivariate way (Van de Ven and Drazin 1985)—that is, a level of the structural variable (e.g., the divisional structure) fits a level of the contingency variable (e.g., the diversification strategy) (Chandler 1962). The level of the contingency variable makes a certain level of the structure the "fitting" level. Information processing theory (Galbraith 1977; Tushman and Nadler 1978) is adopted to explain such a bivariate contingency-structure fit by viewing the fit as the match between the information processing capacity of the structure and the information processing demand of the contingency (Grandori and Furnari 2008).

This bivariate approach can still be valid in a multiple-contingency context (Burton and Obel 1998; Burton et al. 2002, 2003). That is, the fit between one structure and each of its multiple contingencies is identified separately. For example, if formalization has two contingencies, organizational size and environmental uncertainty, then the two fits shall be specified independently: the fit between formalization and organizational size, and the fit between formalization and environmental uncertainty. In this chapter, we define the structural contingency approach as being, in this way, bivariate. That is to say, there is a fit or (misfit) between one contingency and one structural variable, and also a fit (or misfit) between another contingency variable and the same structural variable. For example, there could be an organization whose level of structural formalization is four (out of five) that thereby fits its size contingency of level four (out of five), but simultaneously misfits its environmental uncertainty level of two (out of five).

In this section, we will begin with a framework of multiple-contingency contexts in which three types of contexts and their theoretical implications for the debate are discussed on the basis of Gresov's (1989) insight. Considering the critical role of the relative importance of contingencies, we will offer a critique of Gresov's (1989) criteria of the importance of contingences and provide a new criterion derived from the structural contingency approach. Finally, we will discuss the likelihood of equally important and unequally important contingencies to explore the possibility of equifinality.

A Framework of Multiple-Contingency Contexts

The extant literature has revealed that two dimensions are critical to the multiple-contingency issue: the degree of conflict in the required structure from multiple contingencies and the relative importance of the contingencies. On the one hand, the degree of consistency of the requirements of two contingencies makes a distinction between two contexts: non-conflicting and conflicting contingencies. Many scholars, including Child (1975), Gresov (1989), and Mintzberg (1979), distinguish situations with both non-conflicting and conflicting contingencies in terms of the consistency between the design implications of multiple contingencies for the same structure. Each contingency factor requires the structure to have a certain level to fit it. When these contingencies impose consistent requirements on structure—that is, an equal level of the structural variable—they are non-conflicting contingencies. In contrast, when multiple contingencies have inconsistent implications for the structure—that is, unequal levels of the structure—they are conflicting contingencies. For example, consider the case of formalization fitting two contingencies: organizational size and environmental uncertainty. For a large organization in a stable environment, both its large-size and low-environmental uncertainty (the two contingencies) require its formalization level to be high so that formalization has large-size and low-environmental uncertainty as two non-conflicting contingencies. However, if a large organization is in a highly unstable environment, then its large size requires its formalization level to be high, yet its high uncertainty requires its formalization to be low so that formalization has large size and high uncertainty as two conflicting contingencies.

The relative importance of contingencies also plays a role in the multiple-contingency discussion. This insight from Gresov (1989) distinguishes equally important and unequally important contingencies based on whether or not contingencies are equally relevant to the organizational design. For instance, Gresov (1989, 438) posits that previous concepts of conflicting contingencies "are based on the view that the design imperatives of both contingencies are relatively equal," while it will become a dominant-imperative situation if one contingency is "more important for unit design" than another. Gresov and Drazin (1997) also hold the same logic to distinguish between situations with conflicting and dominant functional demands.

Based primarily on Gresov's (1989) arguments, we develop a framework of multiple-contingency contexts and their respective theoretical implications (see Table 3.1). A cross-classification of the two dimensions discussed earlier—the degree of conflict in the required structure and the importance of contingencies—can create four types of contingency contexts. However, as the two types of contexts with non-conflicting contingencies yield the same implication for organizational design, they are both termed consistent contingencies. Therefore, there are in total three multiple-contingency contexts: consistent contingencies, even contingencies, and dominant contingency.

In Table 3.1, first, when the required structures from multiple contingencies are non-conflicting, it is a *consistent-contingencies* context, no matter

Table 3.1 A Classification of Multiple-Contingency Contexts

		Importance of contingencies	
		Equal	Unequal
Degree of conflict in required structure	Non-conflicting	Consistent contingencies: Single-fitting structure	
	Conflicting	Even contingencies: Equifinality	Dominant contingency: Single-fitting structure

Adapted from Gresov (1989, 435, Figure 1)

whether these contingencies are of equal or unequal importance. In this context, there is a single-fitting structure that fits both of the contingencies. The structural level fitting to one contingency simultaneously fits the other contingency. Hence there is a contingency imperative in this context in that optimal performance comes from fitting the structure to the contingencies by the adoption of the single-structural level that simultaneously fits both contingencies. This holds regardless of whether or not the importance of the multiple contingencies is equal.

In contrast, when the required structures from multiple contingencies are conflicting, if the fit to the contingencies are of equal importance, it is an *even-contingencies* context. Mathematically, the importance of a contingency is measured by b, the effect on performance of the fit of structure to that contingency. The *even-contingencies* context occurs when both contingency fits are equally important—that is, $b_1 = b_2$, where b_1 and b_2 represent the importance of the two contingencies 1 and 2, respectively. In this case, there will be a range of optimal designs available. The structure can fit either one of the contingencies. The levels of the structural variable between these two are also fits. This is shown in Figure 3.2, where the fits of one structure to one contingency lie on the line where the structural level equals the contingency level (Keller 1994). In this zone, the less the structural variable fits one contingency, the more it fits the other contingency, but this is still optimal because the two contingencies are of equal importance (i.e., $b_1 = b_2$).

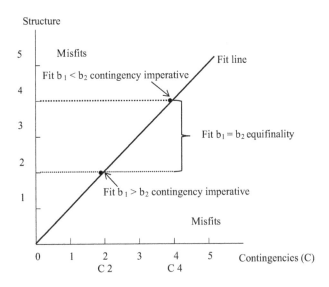

Figure 3.2 Fits to conflicting contingencies in the structural contingency approach

Note: Two is the level of contingency C_1, and four is the level of contingency C_2; b_1 is the effect on performance of the fit of structure to contingency C_1; b_2 is the effect on performance of the fit of structure to contingency C_2.

As an example, in Figure 3.2, if structure is two, then it is a fit to contingency 1 (C_1), Also, if structure is four, then it is a fit to contingency 2 (C_2). Moreover, if structure is three, then it is still a fit because it fits level 3 of the contingencies. This point is one unit less of fit to contingency 1, but one unit more of fit to contingency 2. Hence the performance lost (i.e., $-b$) is *equal* to the performance gained (i.e., $+b$) so that the fit of structural level 3 has the same performance as the fits of structural levels 2 and 4. Thus the fit at structural level 3 lies on the line of fit running between the two fits of structural levels 2 and 4. Thus there is a fitting level of the structure, lying along the fit line, seen between the fits to C_1 and C_2 in Figure 3.2. This would support the equifinality theory in organizational design (Gresov and Drazin 1997) as well as strategic choice theory (Child 1972).

If, however, the required structures from multiple contingencies are conflicting and the contingencies are of *unequal* importance, it is a *dominant-contingency* context (Gresov 1989). This occurs where either the first contingency is more important than the second contingency, i.e., $b_1 > b_2$, or the first contingency is less important than the second contingency, i.e., $b_1 < b_2$. In this situation of unequal importance, there will be a single-fitting structure—that is, the one fitting the more important contingency (Gresov 1989). For example, in Figure 3.2, the structure should fit C_1 when C_1 is more important than C_2 (i.e., $b_1 > b_2$). The reason is because the structural level that fits C_1 is more optimal than the structural level that fits C_2. Also, the structural level that fits C_1 is more optimal than the structural levels between those that fit C_1 and C_2. Similarly, the structure should fit C_2 when C_2 is more important than C_1 (i.e., $b_1 < b_2$). Thus the structure should take one single level, fitting either C_1 or C_2, depending on which is the more important contingency. Hence there is a dominant contingency and so a single-fitting structure (see Figure 3.2). This is compatible with the idea of a contingency imperative.

The aforementioned shows that in conflicting-contingencies contexts, the relative importance of contingencies is critical to determining whether the contingency imperative view is sounder than the equifinality view. Our analysis so far has revealed that, even where the contingencies are conflicting, there can be a dominant contingency and so only one single-fitting structure. Hence there is a contingency imperative *if* the contingencies are unequal in their importance. However, where the contingencies are conflicting, there can be a range of fitting structures and equifinality only *if* the contingencies are equal in their importance. This highlights the concept of the importance of contingencies, which deserves further discussion at this point to explain how it has been conceptualized previously.

A Criterion of the Importance of Contingencies

The earlier discussion showed that the importance of contingencies is critical to the debate between the contingency imperative and equifinality. We suggest that efforts to define the importance of contingencies should refer to the fit concept of structural contingency theory. This section seeks to provide a new criterion of the importance of contingencies that is consistent with structural contingency theory and offers a formalization of the argument.

The identification of a new criterion is derived from the tradition of structural contingency theory. In the structural contingency theory approach to organizational design, the performance implication of fit between structure and a specific factor determines whether this factor is a contingency to the structure (Donaldson 2001; Gresov, Drazin and Van de Ven 1989; Keller 1994; Pennings 1987; Schoonhoven 1981). Only if the fit between structure and a factor causes high performance, and the misfit between them produces low performance, is this factor eligible to be a contingency (Dewar and Werbel 1979; Donaldson 2001; Keller 1994). In this sense, the importance of the contingency should be defined as the effect on performance of the fit between structure and this contingency. The greater the effect on performance of the fit of a structure to a contingency, the more important that contingency is. In other words, the importance of a contingency is reflected by the extent of performance loss resulting from each unit of deviation of the structure from the ideal structure required by this contingency.

Following this new definition of the importance of contingencies, we can say that in the situation of equally important contingencies, the effects on performance of the fits between the structure and each of the multiple contingencies are equal. Conversely, in the circumstance of unequally important contingencies, the effects on performance of the fits between structure and each of the multiple contingencies are not equal.

In the context of conflicting contingencies, the even-contingencies hypothesis suggests that, as fit of structure to any of the contingencies has the same effect on performance, structures that fit any one contingency yet misfit the other would have the same performance and thus are equifinal. In contrast, the dominant-contingency hypothesis implies that, as the fit of the structure to one contingency has a stronger effect on performance than the fit of the structure to the other contingency, the fit to the more important contingency has superior performance, which results in a contingency imperative.

The earlier discussion suggests that, in the contexts of both consistent contingencies and dominant contingency, the contingency imperative view holds. That is, there is only one optimal structure that produces the highest performance: when the levels of multiple contingencies are equal (consistent contingencies) or the importance of multiple contingencies is unequal (dominant contingency). When the required levels of structure from multiple contingencies are non-conflicting (consistent contingencies), the structure fitting one contingency fits another contingency simultaneously. In addition, when the required levels of structure from multiple contingencies are conflicting *and* the importance of these contingencies is unequal (dominant contingency), the structure should fit the more important contingency. Thus in both of these contexts there is a single-fitting structure, hence no equifinality and no zone of strategic choice (Child 1972). Only in the context of even contingencies—that is, when multiple contingencies require conflicting levels of structure and these contingencies are equally important—will there be equifinality, in that organizations achieve equally high performance when the level of S is anywhere between those levels that fit the two contingencies—that is, C_1 and C_2. Only in that situation is there equifinality and strategic choice.

The Likelihood of Equally versus Unequally Important Contingencies

Whether the contingency imperative or equifinality view is more applicable is an empirical issue, as it depends on the likelihood of situations with unequally important or equally important contingencies occurring, respectively. A limited number of prior studies indicate that it is uncommon for multiple contingencies to have equal importance. The effects on performance of fits of structure to different contingencies usually differ. For instance, in his study investigating the relative importance of task uncertainty and horizontal dependence of 529 work units, Gresov (1989) found that for those units revealing significant fit-performance relationships, "design fit was critical to efficiency only if task uncertainty was high. Horizontal dependence appears to have played a secondary role in the fit relationship" (p. 448). It therefore, to a large extent, suggests that task uncertainty is a more important contingency than horizontal dependence on the structures of work units in employment-security offices.

Similarly, Payne (2006) sampled a total of 1,126 medical groups to examine the fitting structural configurations in a suboptimal equifinality context, where quality and efficiency were considered to be two equally important functions that the structure needed to meet. However, his empirical findings showed that structures that fit quality produce superior performance to those that fit efficiency or both quality and efficiency at the same time, in that "Group 1 (the smaller, quality-based organizations) represents the higher-performing configuration type across all performance variables" (p. 764). Hence quality is a more important contingency than efficiency for the design of those medical groups.

Thus, to date, research findings have not supported the idea that two contingencies are usually of equal importance. Prior research provides little evidence for equifinality and free choice of structures. Conversely, the situation where one contingency is more important than the other is more common; i.e., there is a dominant contingency, and as a result, there is usually only one ideal structure. Therefore, the contingency imperative view holds so far in most contexts of multiple-conflicting contingencies.

Structural Separation Approach

The preceding sections argue that equally important contingencies are compatible with equifinality. This section will show that the possibility of equally important contingencies leading to equifinality is further constrained by the availability of structural separation. Only when structural separation is unavailable is equifinality possible. In the structural contingency approach, the structure (or the structural factor) that tends to fit the multiple contingencies is considered as a *whole*. A certain level of the *overall* structure fits multiple contingencies. However, another way to fit the level of structure to the contingency is the structural separation approach (Donaldson 2001; O'Reilly and Tushman 2004; Tushman and O'Reilly 1996). This emphasizes that the fit of the whole structure to multiple contingencies can be realized by having each differentiated *lower-level subsystem* of the structure fit a contingency.

The structural separation approach draws upon the classical differentiation-integration proposition of Lawrence and Lorsch (1967). The idea is that, because the design implication of contingencies differs for different parts of the total structure (Lenz 1981), the organization can be structurally differentiated into multiple parts, each of which is able to cope with the requirement of one contingency. These differentiated units can then be integrated as a whole. By doing so, an organization facing conflicting contingencies simultaneously achieves fits with contradictory demands from multiple contingencies.

The idea of structural separation has been used to address the fit of structure to the conflicting requirements of the same contingency. For instance, because different parts of an organization face different levels of environmental uncertainty, an organization should differentiate itself into multiple subsystems and make each of the subsystems fit the level of uncertainty of its environments and then integrate these subsystems (Lawrence and Lorsch 1967). The following section discusses how structural separation is another way for an organization to fit multiple contingencies simultaneously.

There are generally two types of structural separation, termed in this chapter horizontal and vertical structural separation. Horizontal structural separation is the process of fitting two task contingencies to different parts of the structure at the same level, for example, the work-unit level. This is frequently referred to as structural ambidexterity (O'Reilly and Tushman 2004; Raisch, Birkinshaw, Probst, and Tushman 2009; Tushman and O'Reilly 1996). In contrast, vertical structural separation is the process of fitting different contingencies each at different hierarchical levels. For example, two of the main contingencies of structure are size and task, and vertical structural separation fits them at two different hierarchical levels: administrative and work-unit levels, respectively (Donaldson 2001). In the following sections, we will discuss how structural ambidexterity can resolve the problems of conflicting requirements of multiple task contingencies. Then we will address how vertical structural separation reconciles the contradictory demands of size and task. In relation to the debate between the contingency imperative and equifinality, the structural separation approach will be shown to provide support to the contingency imperative concept. Although there is more than one contingency faced by an organization, each contingency has only one ideal structure that exists in one part of the organization. For the organization as a whole, its fitting structure is the combination of these fitting sub-structures.

Resolution of Conflicting Contingencies by Horizontal Structural Separation

Organizations need to balance exploitation and exploration (March 1991; O'Reilly and Tushman 2004; Tushman and O'Reilly 1996). In the lens of structural contingency theory, we can view exploitation and exploration (Levinthal and March 1993; March 1991) as two contingencies, both of which impose certain requirements on the organizational structure. The requirements for exploitation and exploration are usually conflicting in terms of the requirements for structure. Relatively, exploitation suggests more routine work, while exploration implies more non-routine tasks. In relation to organizational structure, exploitation typically requires a mechanistic structure, while exploration needs an organic structure (Burns and Stalker 1961).

Ambidexterity is the balance of exploration and exploitation (see chapter 4 in this volume) (Binns and Tushman 2016; Tushman and O'Reilly 1996). While there have been various approaches to ambidexterity, including sequential (Brown and Eisenhardt 1997; Nickerson and Zenger 2002) and contextual ambidexterity (Gibson and Birkinshaw 2004; Khazanchi, Lewis, and Boyer 2007), structural ambidexterity is the most relevant to the discussion on equifinality versus the contingency imperative. Such a structural approach to ambidexterity holds that an organization can satisfy the competing demands of exploitation and exploration through structural differentiation and integration (Jansen, Tempelaar, Van Den Bosch, and Volberda 2009; O'Reilly and Tushman 2004; Tushman and O'Reilly 1996; see reviews on this topic in Lavie, Stettner, and Tushman (2010), O'Reilly and Tushman (2013), Raisch and Birkinshaw (2008), and Simsek, Heavey, Veiga, and Souder (2009)). The organization can differentiate itself by having some of its units with a mechanistic structure deal with exploitation tasks, while other units with an organic structure handle exploration tasks. The units can be integrated using integration mechanisms such as senior team shared vision, contingency rewards (Jansen, George, Van den Bosch, and Volberda 2008), social integration, cross-functional interfaces (Burgers and Covin, in press; Jansen et al. 2009), and chief executive officer–top management team interactions (Cao, Simsek, and Zhang 2009).

A good example of an ambidextrous organization is *USA Today*, illustrated in O'Reilly and Tushman (2004). While maintaining its traditional print business, in 1995, *USA Today* also launched an online news service called *USAToday.com*. The old and new businesses represented exploitation and exploration, respectively, and the different units that operated them had "distinctive process, structures, and culture" (O'Reilly and Tushman 2004, 78). Each unit had its own structure and processes that fitted its corresponding task environment, either exploitation or exploration. These differentiated units were intensively integrated through management practices such as a common organizational vision and a common bonus program. *USA Today* was successful in both businesses by adopting two fundamentally different types of structures in its respective business units.

The aforementioned case shows how the organizational structure that resulted from structural separation (and integration) can fit both exploration and exploitation, two equally important contingencies for the survival and success of organizations. One part of the organization with organic structure fits the exploration contingency, and the other part of the organization with mechanistic structure fits the exploitation contingency. Hence, despite facing two equally important contingencies that have different structural fits, they do not conflict, because the organization has one fitting structure that simultaneously accommodates both contingencies to achieve structural ambidexterity. This supports the contingency imperative rather than equifinality.

Resolution of Conflicting Contingencies by Vertical Structural Separation

Task uncertainty and size may make conflicting requirements of the same structural variable (Child 1977; Donaldson 2001). For instance, as task uncertainty increases, the level of formalization should decrease to fit the rate of change in the task environment. In contrast, as size increases, formalization should also increase in order to produce high performance (Child 1975). Thus, for a large organization in a high-uncertainty environment, the required levels of formalization from task uncertainty and size are in conflict.

However, the structure required by task uncertainty and size occurs in different parts of the organization (Donaldson 2001), which is compatible with structural separation. Structural variables required by environmental uncertainty are found in the micro, task-related parts (Burns and Stalker 1961), while the structure fitting to organizational size is related to administrative activities, such as those in the accounting department or in the organization's personnel regulations, as suggested by bureaucratic theory (Blau and Schoenherr 1971; Pugh, Hickson, Hinings, and Turner, 1969). Therefore, the organization can meet the requirements of task uncertainty and size simultaneously through vertical structural separation by coping with high task uncertainty through low formalization levels in innovative tasks, while fitting large size by adopting a high level of formalization in administrative work.

Similar logic of structural separation is also applicable in departmental design. Structural separation or ambidexterity can occur at multiple levels (Simsek 2009), be it in work units or departments (Raisch and Birkinshaw

2008). For example, a large R&D department may fit the requirements for both size and innovation. In order to achieve these objectives simultaneous, the R&D department's administrative activities could be highly standardized at the departmental level, while its R&D work should be low in standardization to facilitate innovation at the level of the project teams and varying according to the uncertainty of the tasks of each team. Thus where structural separation can be used, it provides a solution to conflicting contingencies. For each of the multiple contingencies, it is fitted by only one ideal level of part of the whole structure, which supports the contingency imperative concept.

Moreover, the applicability of the structural separation approach to fitting multiple contingencies is not likely to hinge on the relative importance of contingencies. That is, even when contingencies are conflicting in their levels *and* are equally important, the structural separation approach can still be a feasible solution to multiple contingencies of structure as long as these contingencies have their requirements for different, rather than the same, parts of the structure. Hence, if contingencies are of equal importance, each contingency can still be fitted by one part of the structure. In this case, because each contingency has only one single-fitting structure, the contingency imperative is supported. Hence, even when multiple contingencies are equally important, the structural separation approach still leads to the contingency imperative rather than to equifinality.

Considering the long-standing debate between the contingency imperative and equifinality in the organizational design literature, this chapter sheds new light on some of the points of confusion in this research area. It finds that the contingency imperative is sounder than equifinality and thus reinforces the contingency imperative tradition of structural contingency theory. It can be viewed as an explanation of why, although equifinality was highlighted as one of the missed research opportunities in organization theory (Ashmos and Huber 1987), so far not much evidence for equifinality has been found (Sinha and Van de Ven 2005; Van de Ven et al. 2013). It may suggest that further research effort in the field of organizational design, to be more fruitful, should probably follow the contingency imperative tradition of structural contingency theory rather than equifinality.

Conclusion

This chapter addresses the debate within organizational theory between the contingency imperative and equifinality in the context of multiple contingencies. It shows that the contingency imperative is valid in the most common contexts, whereas equifinality is only applicable when contingencies are uneven in their levels and equally important. Moreover, even when both of these conditions hold, if the structural separation approach (using the differentiation and integration of the structure to fit multiple contingencies) is available, then each contingency can be fitted using one single level of a sub-structure, which supports the contingency imperative. In sum, there is usually a contingency imperative for a structure to fit multiple contingencies, because either structural separation holds, or there is a dominant contingency, or the levels of the contingencies are even. Thus the idea of equifinality in fitting to multiple contingencies becomes less likely in practice, and the concept of the contingency imperative is more likely to apply in practice.

Note

1 This research is supported by the Fundamental Research Funds for the Central Universities, and the Research Funds of Renmin University of China (14XNF023).

References

Ashmos, D. P. and G. P. Huber. 1987. The systems paradigm in organization theory: Correcting the record and suggesting the future. *Academy of Management Review* 12:607–21.

Binns, A. and M. Tushman. 2016. Getting started with ambidexterity. In *Advancing organizational theory in a complex world*. Qiu, J. XJ, B. N. Luo, C. Jackson, and K. Sanders, eds. New York: Routledge.

Birkinshaw, J., R. Nobel, and J. Ridderstrale. 2002. Knowledge as a contingency variable: Do the characteristics of knowledge predict organization structure? *Organization Science* 13:274–89.

Blau, P. M. and P. A. Schoenherr. 1971. *The structure of organizations*. New York: Basic Books.

Brown, S. L. and K. M. Eisenhardt. 1997. The art of continuous change: Linking complexity theory and time-based evolution in relentlessly shifting organizations. *Administrative Science Quarterly* 42:1–34.

Burgers, J. H. and J. G. Covin (2016). The contingent effects of differentiation and integration on corporate entrepreneurship. *Strategic Management Journal, 37,* 521–540.

Burns, T. and G. M. Stalker. 1961. *The management of innovation*. London, UK: Tavistock.

Burton, R. M., G. Desanctis, and B. Obel. 2006. *Organizational design: A step-by-step approach*. Cambridge and New York: Cambridge University Press.

Burton, R. M., J. Lauridsen, and B. Obel. 2002. Return on assets loss from situational and contingency misfits. *Management Science* 48:1461–85.

Burton, R. M., J. Lauridsen, and B. Obel. 2003. Erratum: Return on assets loss from situational and contingency misfits. *Management Science* 49:1119.

Burton, R. M. and B. Obel.1998. *Strategic organizational diagnosis and design: Developing theory for application*. Boston, MA: Kluwer Academic Publishers.

Burton, R., B. Obel, and D. D. Håkonsson. 2016. Contingency theory, dynamic fit, and contracts. In *Advancing organizational theory in a complex world*. Qiu, J. XJ, B. N. Luo, C. Jackson, and K. Sanders, eds. New York: Routledge.

Cao, Q., Z. Simsek, and H. Zhang. 2009. Modelling the joint impact of the CEO and the TMT on organizational ambidexterity. *Journal of Management Studies* 47:1272–96.

Carroll, T. N., T. J. Gormley, V. J. Bilardo, R. M. Burton, and K. L. Woodman. 2006. Designing a new organization at NASA: An organization design process using simulation. *Organization Science* 17:202–14.

Chandler, Jr., A. D. 1962. *Strategy and structure: Chapters in the history of the industrial enterprise.* Cambridge: MIT Press.

Child, J. 1972. Organization structure and strategies of control: A replication of the Aston study. *Administrative Science Quarterly* 17:163–77.

Child, J. 1975. Managerial and organizational factors associated with company performance, part 2: A contingency analysis. *Journal of Management Studies* 12:12–27.

Child, J. 1977. Organizational design and performance: Contingency theory and beyond. *Organization and Administrative Sciences* 8:169–83.

Child, J. 1984. *Organization: A guide to problems and practice.* London, UK: Harper and Row.

Dewar, R. and J. Werbel. 1979. Universalistic and contingency predictions of employee satisfaction and conflict. *Administrative Science Quarterly* 24:426–48.

Donaldson, L. 1982. Comments on 'contingency and choice in organization theory.' *Organization Studies* 3:65–72.

Donaldson, L. 1985. *In defence of organization theory: A reply to the critics.* Cambridge, UK: Cambridge University Press.

Donaldson, L. 1987. Strategy and structural adjustment to regain fit and performance: In defence of contingency theory. *Journal of Management Studies* 24:1–24.

Donaldson, L. 2001. *The contingency theory of organizations.* Thousand Oaks, CA: Sage.

Doty, D. H., W. H. Glick, and G. P. Huber. 1993. Fit, equifinality, and organizational effectiveness: A test of two configurational theories. *Academy of Management Journal* 36:1196–1250.

Drazin, R. and A. H. Van De Ven. 1985. Alternative forms of fit in contingency theory. *Administrative Science Quarterly* 30:514–39.

Egelhoff, W. G. and J. Wolf. 2016. Building higher-level contingency theory to reconcile contradictions between lower-level theories. In *Advancing organizational theory in a complex world.* Qiu, J. XJ, B. N. Luo, C. Jackson, and K. Sanders, eds. New York: Routledge.

Galbraith, J. R.1977. *Organization design.* Reading, MA: Addison-Wesley.

Gibson, C. B. and J. Birkinshaw. 2004. The antecedents, consequences, and mediating role of organizational ambidexterity. *Academy of Management Journal* 47:209–26.

Grandori, A. and S. Furnari. 2008. A chemistry of organization: combinatory analysis and design. *Organization Studies* 29:459–85.

Gresov, C. 1989. Exploring fit and misfit with multiple contingencies. *Administrative Science Quarterly* 34:431–53.

Gresov, C. 1990. Effects of dependence and tasks on unit design and efficiency. *Organization Studies* 11:503–29.

Gresov, C. and R. Drazin. 1997. Equifinality: Functional equivalence in organization design. *Academy of Management Review* 22:403–28.

Gresov, C., R. Drazin, and A. H. Van De Ven. 1989. Work-unit task uncertainty, design and morale. *Organization Studies* 10:45–62.

Hage, J. 1965. An axiomatic theory of organizations. *Administrative Science Quarterly* 10:289–320.

Hollenbeck, J. R., H. Moon, A. P. J. Ellis, B. J. West, D. R. Ilgen, L. Sheppard, C. O. L. H. Porter, and J. A. Wagner III. 2002. Structural contingency theory and individual differences: Examination of external and internal person–team fit. *Journal of Applied Psychology* 87:599–606.

Jansen, J. J. P., G. George, F. A. J. Van Den Bosch, and H. W. Volberda. 2008. Senior team attributes and organizational ambidexterity: The moderating role of transformational leadership. *Journal of Management Studies* 45:982–1007.

Jansen, J. J. P., M. P. Tempelaar, F. A. J. Van Den Bosch, and H. W. Volberda. 2009. Structural differentiation and ambidexterity: The mediating role of integration mechanisms. *Organization Science* 20:797–811.

Jennings, D. F. and S. L. Seaman. 1994. High and low levels of organizational adaptation: An empirical analysis of strategy, structure, and performance. *Strategic Management Journal* 15:459–75.

Kang, S. C. and S. A. Snell. 2009. Intellectual capital architectures and ambidextrous learning: A framework for human resource management. *Journal of Management Studies* 46:65–92.

Katz, D. and R. L. Kahn. 1966. *The social psychology of organizations.* New York: John Wiley and Sons.

Keller, R. T. 1994. Technology-information processing fit and the performance of R&D project groups: A test of contingency theory. *Academy of Management Journal* 37:167–79.

Khazanchi, S., M. W. Lewis, and K. K. Boyer. 2007. Innovation-supportive culture: The impact of organizational values on process innovation. *Journal of Operations Management* 25:871–84.

Klaas, P. and J. Lauridsen. 2016. Structural adaptation to regain fit: Multiple misfits and structural complexity. In *Advancing organizational theory in a complex world.* Qiu, J. XJ, B. N. Luo, C. Jackson, and K. Sanders, eds. New York: Routledge.

Klaas, P., J. Lauridsen, and D. D. Håkonsson. 2006. New developments in contingency fit theory. In *Organizational design: The evolving state-of-the-art.* Burton, R. M., B. Eriksen, D. D. Håkonsson, and C. C. Snow, eds. New York, NY: Springer.

Lavie, D., U. Stettner, and M. L. Tushman. 2010. Exploration and exploitation within and across organizations. *Academy of Management Annals* 4:109–55.

Lawrence, P. R. and J. W. Lorsch. 1967. Differentiation and integration in complex organizations. *Administrative Science Quarterly* 12:1–47.

Lenz, R. T. 1981. Determinants of organizational performance: An interdisciplinary review. *Strategic Management Journal* 2:131–54.

Levinthal, D. A. and J. G. March. 1993. The myopia of learning. *Strategic Management Journal* 14:95–112.

March, J. G. 1991. Exploration and exploitation in organizational learning. *Organization Science* 2:71–87.

Miller, D. 1992. Environmental fit versus internal fit. *Organization Science* 3:159–78.

Mintzberg, H. 1979. An emerging strategy of "direct" research. *Administrative Science Quarterly* 24:582–89.

Nickerson, J. and T. Zenger. 2002. Being efficiently fickle: A dynamic theory of organizational choice. *Organization Science* 13:547–66.

O'Reilly, C. A. and M. L. Tushman. 2004. The ambidextrous organization. *Harvard Business Review*, April, 74–83.

O'Reilly, C. A. and M. L. Tushman. 2013. Organizational ambidexterity: Past, present, and future. *Academy of Management Perspectives* 27:324–38.

Payne, G. T. 2006. Examining configurations and firm performance in a suboptimal equifinality context. *Organization Science* 17:756–70.

Pennings, J. M. 1987. Structural contingency theory: A multivariate test. *Organization Studies* 8:223–40.

Perrow, C. 1967. A framework for the comparative analysis of organizations. *American Sociological Review* 32:194–208.

Pugh, D. S., D. J. Hickson, C. R. Hinings, and C. Turner. 1968. Dimensions of organization structure. *Administrative Science Quarterly* 13, 65–105.

Pugh, D. S., D. J. Hickson, C. R. Hinings, and C. Turner. 1969. The context of organization structures. *Administrative Science Quarterly* 14:91–114.

Raisch, S. and J. Birkinshaw. 2008. Organizational ambidexterity: Antecedents, outcomes, and moderators. *Journal of Management* 34:375–409.

Raisch, S., J. Birkinshaw, G. Probst, and M. L. Tushman. 2009. Organizational ambidexterity: Balancing exploitation and exploration for sustained performance. *Organization Science* 20:685–95.

Rumelt, R. P. 1974. *Strategy, structure and economic performance.* Boston: Harvard University, Graduate School of Business Administration, Division of Research.

Schoonhoven, C. B. 1981. Problems with contingency theory: Testing assumptions hidden within the language of contingency "theory". *Administrative Science Quarterly* 26:349–77.

Simsek, Z. 2009. Organizational ambidexterity: Toward a multilevel understanding. *Journal of Management Studies* 46:597–624.

Simsek, Z., C. Heavey, J. F. Veiga, and D. Souder. 2009. A typology for aligning organizational ambidexterity's conceptualizations, antecedents, and outcomes. *Journal of Management Studies* 46:864–94.

Sinha, K. K. and A. H. Van de Ven. 2005. Designing work within and between organizations. *Organization Science* 16:389–408.

Thompson, J. D. 1967. *Organizations in action.* New York: McGraw-Hill.

Tushman, M. L. and D. A. Nadler. 1978. Information processing as an integrating concept in organizational design. *Academy of Management Review* 3:613–24.

Tushman, M. L. and C. A. O'Reilly. 1996. Ambidextrous organizations: Managing evolutionary and revolutionary change. *California Management Review* 38:8–30.

Van de Ven, A. H. and R. Drazin. 1985. The concept of fit in contingency theory. In *Research in organizational behavior.* Staw, B. M. and L. L. Cummings, eds. Vol. 7. Greenwich, CT: JAI Press, 333–65.

Van de Ven, A. H., M. Ganco, and C. R. Hinings. 2013. Returning to the frontier of contingency theory of organizational and institutional designs. *Academy of Management Annals* 7:393–440.

Van de Ven, A. H., R. Leung, J. P. Bechara, and K. Sun. 2012. Changing organizational designs and performance frontiers. *Organization Science* 23:1055–76.

Van Offenbeek, M., A. Sorge, and M. Knip. 2009. Enacting fit in work organization and occupational structure design: The case of intermediary occupations in a Dutch hospital. *Organization Studies* 30:1083–1114.

Volberda, H. W., N. Van Der Weerdt, E. Verwaal, M. Stienstra, and A. J. Verdu. 2012. Contingency fit, institutional fit, and firm performance: A metafit approach to organization–environment relationships. *Organization Science* 23:1040–54.

von Bertalanffy, L. 1968. *General system theory.* New York: Braziller.

Wasserman, N. 2008. Revisiting the strategy, structure, and performance paradigm: The case of venture capital. *Organization Science* 19:241–59.

Woodward, J. 1965. *Industrial organization: Theory and practice.* Oxford, UK: Oxford University Press.

4 Getting Started with Ambidexterity

Andrew Binns and Michael Tushman[1]

Ambidexterity is an established answer to the question of how firms can manage the tensions of "exploring" into new areas at the same time as "exploiting" existing business models.[2] The ambidextrous organizational form separates out these two sets of activities into distinct units, each with the flexibility to adapt key decisions on people, culture, skills, and processes to the needs of the specific business strategy. At the same time, the exploratory unit is not a spinout and retains "targeted integration" with the core business. Such targeted structural integration in the context of senior team integration permits the incumbent to leverage the assets of the firm in its exploratory experiments and facilitates taking the new business to scale if it matures. In service of both exploring and exploiting, structural ambidexterity is based on a different logic than traditional contingency theory of differentiation and integration.[3] Structural ambidexterity ideas are anchored in the notion of high differentiation, targeted (i.e., limited) structural integration, and strong senior team integration.[4]

There are several high-profile cases of successful application of the principles of ambidexterity, most notably IBM's Emerging Business Opportunity program. A range of firms have grown new businesses consistent with ambidextrous principles, such as Ciba-Geigy (now Novartis), Gannett Corporation, and LexisNexis. Tushman and O'Reilly detail these cases, the success factors associated with them, and the steps necessary to manage a transition to this form of organizational leadership.[5]

However, in reality, relatively few firms successfully adopt the ambidextrous model, citing the "risk aversion" of publicly traded companies and the difficulty of attachment to existing business models as primary reasons for this failure.[6] From our comparison of more versus less successful implementation of ambidextrous designs, we suggest that there are "three moments" around which ambidexterity turns—ideation, incubation, and scaling. *Ideation* involves generating ideas for potential new businesses. *Incubation* is about nurturing the idea before committing resources. *Scaling* converts the verified concept into a viable business that is differentiated from the core business unit, though sufficiently integrated to leverage its assets. Scaling is the primary focus for the literature on the ambidextrous organization.[7] Our hypothesis for the relatively few successful ambidextrous organizations is that there is a breakdown in the "incubation" phase so that promising ideas do not progress.

This led us to initiate a research study to understand better how firms "get started" with ambidexterity. We interviewed executives at the corporate level of 17 publicly traded and 3 private companies; and, the business-unit level of a further 6 public firms. Of these 26 firms, most were headquartered in the United States and in the technology and media sectors, though our sample includes two financial services firms, three business services firms, and a manufacturing company. The organization's names are disguised to respect anonymity. In a number of cases, we have drawn on other research or examples from our consulting practice to illustrate findings derived from the research.

Each of the companies had attempted to develop and launch at least one new business venture. In total, there were 35 new ventures across 26 firms. We asked interviewees to assess the success of the ventures relative to initial expectations as well as outcome measures such as revenue and milestone accomplishment (e.g., customer adoption). Nine of the 35 were reported as entirely or mostly successful, and the rest fell below expectations or failed.

Our research[8] broadly supported our hypothesis that the breakdown occurs at the "incubation" moment. In this paper, we seek to examine why innovations are rejected so early in their development. With these data, we recommend several key success factors for improving the probability of success. These recommendations are largely based on the practices of the innovations that discriminated between more versus less successful movement from experimentation into a fully scaled, ambidextrous unit. We conclude that corporations seeking to get started with ambidexterity should

1   *Understand the nature of the innovation*: Validated experiments need to transition from unproven concept to "exploratory business" with full-time staff and resources separated out as an ambidextrous unit. This is a key point of vulnerability, not addressed by the "start-up" inspired methodologies.

2   *Identify risk of the innovation being "toxic" to the core*: Venturing outside the core business, particularly into areas of new opportunity, frequently involves challenging the assumptions, and norms, of the traditional business. Experiments remain highly vulnerable to this toxicity, even when managed as an experiment.

3   *Adopt a "business experimentation" approach to manage incubation moment*: Based on models from the world of "venture-backed start-ups," this approach seeks to validate the new business opportunity with carefully designed experiments that test each element of the value proposition before committing resources to scale the new unit.

4   *Apply key success factors for business experiments*: Having described the principal features of business experimentation, we then describe the

practices that differentiate successful from unsuccessful applications of the method in the large enterprise context. We formulate these into eight "key success factors."

Understand the Nature of the Innovation

Any new innovation must first be understood with respect to the core business, specifically to understand (i) is the innovation addressing current or new customer groups, (ii) are the capabilities required to execute the innovation incremental or new, and (iii) does the innovation substitute for an existing revenue stream within the firm? The first step in answering these questions is to plot the "innovation streams" (Figure 4.1) of a particular firm against a simple two-by-two model. The map is built from the point of view of the company's current core business. The y-axis plots the markets served by the company—does the innovation meet current or new market needs—and the x-axis plots the capabilities comprising the offering (product or service) with respect to the firm's existing product or service. Each sector of the model has a different implication, which helps a company to sense a market shift, understand its potential implications, and prepare a response.

- *Incremental improvement to existing offerings or current customers*: This is the art of constantly improving on the product/service from which you are already generating profits. Apple has iterated its original

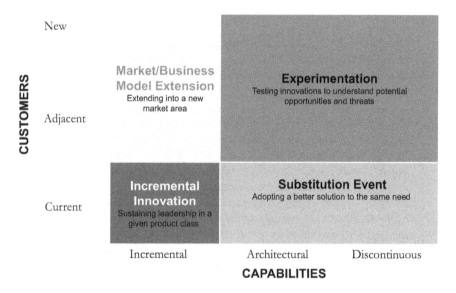

Figure 4.1 Innovation streams

iPod through multiple generations by updating the functionality, reducing the size, and lowering the cost. Incremental innovations are properly the domain of the current business unit, the risk of "toxicity" is low, and it is most likely that it will bring the new business to scale quickly.

- *Market extensions*: Serving new customers with existing capabilities involves doing what a firm knows how to do for adjacent markets. Wal-Mart has mastered this capability by generating multiple retail formats across the globe to penetrate distinct markets. These are frequently subunits of the existing business that enjoy some degree of separation from the core but within the same operational model. This permits a more coherent expansion of the business sharing go-to-market and supply-chain assets. In our research, a logistics company took its core competence of moving large volumes of industrial equipment and transferred it to supplying consumables to offices. Its IT systems and trucks were identical, though there was a shift in the customer need it served. Although there was contention at the senior team level over how to resource the new venture, it was within a known area of competence for the firm, and so it was able to sustain support for investment.

- *Substitution events*: Serving existing market requirements with new capabilities. These are often radical events that lead to the displacement of the incumbent. Local newspapers in the United States were displaced when advertisers moved listings to free online services. It made no difference to the fate of local newspapers that they introduced color advertising and better printing presses (incremental) when the search for local listing information went to Craigslist (substitution). These are the most difficult decisions to make as customers overlap, so a separate unit will introduce the risk of channel conflict. Integrating a substitution within the core leaves it exposed to toxicity of the firms' traditional competencies and business model. The approach that appears to correlate best with success is to have some form of corporate-level ambidexterity. One successful example from our research is the information management firm that separated out a development team at the corporate level to build a product platform that would entirely replace its core product offering. This was then merged with the business unit so that it could migrate customers to the new platform. Elsewhere, we have written about IBM's Emerging Business Opportunities, which were "housed" within a business unit, but had a direct reporting line to a board-level sponsor who provided "air cover" to ensure that they were successful.

- *Disruption*: New capabilities to serve new or emerging market requirements are often made possible by those capabilities. The iPhone displaced from the market mobile phones, digital personal assistants, and personal music devices. These innovations are unquestionably the domain of an ambidextrous unit that needs to have differentiation from the core sufficient to adapt to the unique needs of its market. It also requires integration so that it can leverage the product, go-to-market, technology, and infrastructure assets of the core.

The data from this assessment inform a judgment about the best way to manage an innovation. Incremental innovations and most market extensions are best advanced by the core business, which has the motivation and assets to maximize the potential of new revenue streams. Innovations that sit in the substitution or disruption quadrants require another level of analysis to identify the risk of them being "toxic" to the core business and the likelihood of being rejected.

Identify Risk of the Innovation Being "Toxic" to the Core

Substitutions and disruptive innovations often involve a firm learning about areas beyond its core competencies. This was common to many of our companies in the study; for example, a semiconductor firm learned to derive value from software algorithms as well as from selling microprocessors. This involved software improving the functioning of an integrated circuit. These software innovations displaced both the dominant hardware skill base of electrical engineers in the firm and the business model associated with selling silicon chips. Another firm was a broadcast television content producer that was making a shift into digital media, where the TV studios, production qualities, and artistic skills were entirely different. Or, a US bank that developed a new service to enable consumers to manage personal healthcare expenses, where the money-making model was subscription based rather than the deposits, interests, and charges per the traditional banking model. In each of these cases, the innovations challenged assumptions of either the existing business model or basis of competence of the firm. They were "toxic" to the traditional business, and if the assumptions of the core were applied in running them, it would kill the experiment.

The risk of "toxicity" to the core, or competence destruction, is best understood through a case study example. Between 2005 and 2010, the market for recorded music fell by a quarter as "physical" formats—records, tapes, CDs—were replaced by digital downloads and streaming. Recording companies suffered severely, as did many recording artists. The market for live musical entertainment though, actually tripled between 1999 and 2009 from $1.5 billion to $4.6 billion—vastly exceeding the growth of inflation and population growth. The trick for any band is how to fill the venue without already having a record deal with which to build a following. One band that solved this challenge was OK Go. They pioneered by using YouTube to post their music videos—for example, running on a treadmill as they sang—to build a fan base. The video went viral, and they became a hit band capable of filling large stadia. OK Go built a new way to generate a fan base that allowed them to adopt a disruptive business model based on ticket sales from live shows, not a recording contract.

At the same time, the record company EMI was close to bankruptcy and vigorously pursuing opportunities to establish growing revenue streams based on digital and live shows. In 2008, EMI signed OK Go to a recording contract, which reflected the band's popularity and the record label's desire to enter the new world of entertainment. They were starting to see that "music is getting harder to define . . . it is becoming less of an object and more of an experience,"[9] and so their new signing gave them an entry into the new world of live entertainment. OK Go benefited with a recording contract, distribution deal, and investment in the video content that made them so distinctive. They also got something they hadn't expected: a new set of rules for how the online content could be used, i.e., do not post for free on the web. In other words, no ability to post the video on blogs, Facebook, and other social media outlets; it was a denial of the fundamental premise of their business model. OK Go resigned from EMI in 2010. More broadly, EMI had trouble finding where and how to add value in this web-mediated music environment. EMI was liquidated in 2012. The assumptions of its past business model were toxic to its future one. Just as EMI reached for the future, it was unable to grasp how making money in the new world was different from the old.

In our research, we identified this as a persistent cause of failure in the setting up of a new exploratory growth business. Firms failed to understand how the competencies of the core business had embedded within them ways of working that were corrosive to the success of the new venture. These assumptions were typically represented in business processes, organizational arrangements, people skills, or behavioral norms. For example, in the aftermath of 9/11, a highly successful US defense contractor made a decision to take its existing competence in securing the perimeters of defense establishments and make it available to non-military sites. The firm excelled at developing high-technology solutions for a range of issues in the "homeland security" market and won national awards in some cases. They provided appropriate marketing and bid preparation resources based on the template of their existing US Defense Department contracts and sought to win contracts in the new market. Unfortunately, its potential buyers were individual cities, ports, and airports across the United States and far more fragmented than its traditional market and significantly more cost sensitive.

The innovation needs to be managed to insulate it from sources of "toxicity," without removing it so far from the core business that it is unable to leverage the advantages that being a part of a large successful organization can bring. Innovations struggle to defend themselves against the toxicity of the core because they are, by nature, uncertain and unproven. For example, the two semiconductor firms in our study are managing uncertainties created by the so-called Internet of Things: an emerging trend in technology that promises to transform multiple industries by connecting devices, appliances, and machines. There are few actual new business models in this realm—though the forecast value of the market by 2020 is in the trillions of US dollars.[10] They need to manage the uncertainty and find ways to lead the emerging market rather than find themselves disrupted by new entrants.

All firms in our sample referred to "risk aversion" as a core inhibitor in these situations; a firm will dare not risk too much investment in the unknown at the expense of predictable returns from the core. Firms described a history of pursuing uncertain market opportunities by doing just enough to participate, but not so much that a failure would risk quarterly business performance. This "under commitment" was an attempt to hedge against disruptive new technologies and business models, but rarely led to a firm building a scalable position in a new market. On the flip side, some had made an *over-commitment* to a new business area and spent ahead of evidence that there was a valid business opportunity to pursue. In one case, the CEO spoke of "burning the bridges" to the past business model and dedicated the firm's entire R&D budget to an unproven technology.

Adopt a "Business Experimentation" Approach to Manage Incubation Moment

Our research identified that those more successful firms resolved this dichotomy by adopting a discipline of structuring new ventures as *business experiments*. There is a proliferation of models and approaches advocated as a means for managing such experiments and all are derived from the experiences of start-up companies. These include Steve Blank's "Customer Discovery Model,"[11] Eric Reis's "Lean Start-Up" approach,[12] and Stanford Design School's "Design Thinking" approach.[13] We found no single methodology in use across the sample of firms. Although some mentioned "Lean Start-Up" and "Design Thinking," only two described a conscious attempt to apply the methodologies. Some version of an "experiment" methodology was discernable in 18 of our 26 firms and present in all but one of our success cases. Common across these companies was the use of three or more of the following elements, which we are calling a "business experiment":

1   *Customer insight*: It starts with a problem in the world rather than a solution in the labs. Experiments focus on solving a customer problem, or "use case," rather than testing the applicability of different technologies to different markets. For example, the television production company in our sample created content exclusively in Spanish for US Hispanics. It observed that increasing numbers of US Hispanics prefer to speak English, but prefer classic Latin American television formats (e.g., telenovelas). There was a clear problem in the world.

2   *Value proposition hypothesis*: A solution to the identified problem that will satisfy a wide enough group of potential customers to enable an innovator to make money by delivering that value. In our television company example, they designed experiments to test a value proposition for telenovelas in English.

3   *Early prototyping*: Solutions to identified customer problems are "mocked up" in "minimal" versions that enable hypotheses about the features and functionality required to deliver the value proposition to be verified empirically with potential customers. In the television example, this involved scripts, trial scenes, and treatments to sell to broadcasters that might distribute the content.

4   *Test and iteration cycles*: This prototyping feeds a cycle of iteration, whereby the solution is adapted and tested repeatedly to refine the design. Revisions to the television show scripts, situations, and actors were made in the telenovela experiment to make the proposition a better fit for its market.

5   *Evidence-based exploration*: The experimental approach regards every aspect of the proposed business as a "hypothesis" to be proven or disproved; the assumption is that learning through doing yields a more valid answer in an area of uncertainty than traditional strategic analysis.

Given that use of some number of these elements of the "business experiment" were discernable across the sample, we decided to explore what might explain some or all of the variance in performance across the experiments. We identified eight potential key success factors that appear to be core to applying the "experiments" approach within the corporate (i.e., not venture-backed start-up) context.

Apply Key Success Factors for Business Experiments in Corporations

The first key success factor is to *set an appropriate scale of ambition* (KSF#1). New ventures are by definition less certain and take longer to payback on an investment. This creates a challenge for mature organizations that are used to assessing risk and return with a higher degree of confidence in the core business. This contributes to the paradox of over-committing and under-committing to which we've already referred. It is rational for an experiment to under-commit to reduce the risk of under-delivering. However, that may also mean under-investing relative to the market opportunity. One technology firm in our sample identified that its investment in new product innovation had increased by a third in the past decade, even as its revenue from new products had dropped alarmingly. Detailed analysis revealed how more projects were being funded, but all at the minimum amount to sustain activity. Although funding innovation, they had not set a high enough level of ambition for any one project and then made a decision to fund it. In other examples, the scale of ambition is unrealistically high, and often not tied to a performance outcome; e.g., "we are going to reinvent the insurance industry." Choosing an "appropriate" level of ambition means to stretch to the scale of the market opportunity, while at the same time having specific, tangible goals.

One consequence of not having clear goals is that the progress of the "experiment" cannot be assessed. In the case of a financial services company, a team charged with leading a new business investment found that not only were they underfunded, but there were also no mechanisms for holding it accountable for what it spent. The impact of this was that the project leader had no mechanism for demonstrating progress toward her goal. This is why it is vital to establish a *feedforward management system* (KSF#2) to support the new experiments.

Most organizations work on the basis of reviewing data on past performance relative to expectations and then taking action to correct errors. This is a feedback loop: what was our goal, how did we do, what explains the variance, take action to close the gap. What's required for an experiment is a feedforward system that tracks performance toward an aspiration using milestone-based measures to understand how an experiment is performing relative to its hypotheses. For example, one semiconductor firm adopted a system by which all new business investments had to define "early success factors." These were achievements that they would have on the path toward the ultimate goal for the experiment. These included milestones, such as having a viable prototype, and lead indicators, such as the number of customer adoptions of the technical design.

These systems for increasing transparency of performance milestones help engage *senior management teams with the experiments* (KSF#3). The role of senior management teams in ensuring the success of ambidexterity is well documented elsewhere.[14] That role is just as vital in the experimentation phase, though necessarily it is less intensive than at a later stage when there is a validated business model. In more than half of our failure cases, senior leaders played little or no role in sponsoring the experiment, or there was explicit disagreement in the senior team over the viability of the effort. In two cases, there was tension between organic and inorganic routes to growth that prevented support for the experiments in the senior team. The argument was that innovation was best pursued through an acquisition strategy rather than as a part of an internal effort. This disagreement caused both projects to be closed down in response to negative data from the initial experiments. Because of the lack of alignment in the senior team over what the experiment's objective and the means for assessing its success (i.e., feedforward) would be, it was without support at a critical moment. In a contrasting example, the leadership team of a $1 billion media firm invested eight days over six months in setting the strategic context for their $200 million experiments portfolio. Given this extensive work in advance, this firm executed at pace with positive market feedback.

We also found that those more effective senior teams *split meetings between core business and experiments so that they could tailor their styles of engagement* (KSF#4). Most businesses adopt a quarterly business or operation review meeting cadence that involves a ritual of examining data about past and forecast business performance. Each firm has its distinctive culture, but they are frequently associated with management style in which errors are punished. This may be appropriate in a business with a known operating rhythm in which variances can be explained and corrected. However, with an uncertain, unproven business in which you are verifying hypotheses, failure teaches you what not to do; it's a positive, as it prevents you from investing in areas that are not valued by customers.

One of our successful firms chose to split its management system into two distinct processes. The first is the existing rigorous quarterly business review at which current contracts are examined for margin contribution and revenue forecasts, and there is an intense focus on every number. The second they called a "Horizons Review," borrowing from the popular notion of "Three Horizons of Growth."[15] This review process was different in content and approach. It was less formal, more oriented toward learning from mistakes, and deliberately future oriented. It included reviews of current experiments, performance of units that had been funded to scale, and briefings on long-term market trends. The design is deliberately loose to contrast it with the tightness of the Quarterly Business Reviews (QBRs). The meetings have a different location, seating plan, and agenda to reflect the focus on diversity of thinking. They use the Horizons Review to hold the new ventures accountable, make decisions on what to fund and what to kill off, and solicit future ideas. This approach enabled them to give equal attention to the day-to-day operations of the business, in their "QBR" process, and to the future of the firm.

Another firm has adopted a venture capital "shark-tank" style approach to funding new ventures in which teams have ten minutes to pitch an idea for funding or to update on an existing experiment in search of another round of investment. These mechanisms break the established operating rituals of the business act to speed up decision making and to give senior management the opportunity to provide constructive feedback to the teams involved.

A fifth key success factor reflects the volunteer nature of experimental efforts. *Experiments need to be formally scoped with explicit agreements on what will be achieved by when (KSF#5).* The mythology of the Google or HP "garage start-up" is very strong and leads some to conclude that experiments should be defined by informality. Several firms in our study have redesigned workspaces to support a "start-up" atmosphere and attract younger talent with digital skills. However, informality does not need to mean lack of clarity on what the experiment is seeking to test. The more successful experiments adopt a common language for the areas in which they need to formulate hypotheses—using, for example, a "business design" template or the more recent "strategy canvas" tool.[16] One media firm created a methodology with cross-functional teams from across the business in which each focused on a specific experiment. Each team had a process to follow in strict 90-day cycles, support from an external facilitator, and a clear set of expectations from the senior team. This contributed to their success converting several experiments into revenue-generating businesses.[17]

One common strategy for entering a new market is to hire an executive from outside the firm to bring expertise, knowledge, and capabilities the firm lacks. Eleven of our interviewees were appointed to lead innovation units or projects at the experimental stage from outside the firm. They accounted for a disproportionate number of the failed projects: 9 of the 11. This confirms other research that suggests the "external appointment" approach correlates with underperformance in ambidextrous units.[18] Our sixth key success factor is to *choose an insider/outsider combination to lead experiments* (KSF#6). What was clear is that insiders have a social network to leverage inside the organization that enables them to call in favors, leverage assets outsiders don't know, and manage skeptical stakeholders who might otherwise seek to shut the project down. One successful outsider in a Japanese-owned technology firm explained how he had built a deep personal network across the firm before making any moves. He waited two years before he brought forward a plan for new business experiments.

In contrast, an experienced financial services marketing executive was hired from the outside to lead new business creation at a credit card issuing company. She described how the core business made no effort to actively oppose her efforts. However, they denied her any support and assistance; she described it as "trekking through the Amazon with a butter knife." Her team was under-equipped to achieve its goals and could not get access to the resources of the core business. She described how her team became isolated in its approach—"we became the rebel alliance"—and totally failed to build the relationships they needed to be successful. The executive admits this reflected her own need to grow as a leader. However, the example does support the conclusion that having a leader with "social capital" within an organization on which they can draw is critical to success. If possible, a combination of leaders who in partnership bring internal knowledge and credit, as well as external points of view and relevant skills, may best reflect the needs of business at the experiment stage.

Appointing an "innovation leader" with responsibility for designing and overseeing experiments did correlate with success in most cases, particularly when this leader was an "insider" with social capital. The successful incumbents in this role are able to *engage the organization in the work through a voluntary task-force approach.* (KSF#7) Most firms rely on some element of volunteerism in completing experiments, although there are full-time resources, most early stage ventures rely on squeezing out resources from existing activities. Experiments are too small to justify the expense of a separate business unit.

The innovation leader, though, can organize his or her volunteer resources in different ways. One technology firm uses a rotational model, with marketers and engineers spending one to two years working part-time on projects with the "innovation garage." The television production company adopted a task-force model that launched teams on 90-day *sprints* to test and validate new business models. One European financial services firm has sent more than 40 senior executives to *innovation programs* at six different business schools around the globe. The logic is that the diversity of experience will encourage a culture of innovation at the firm. It is so far uncertain whether this approach is effective; one risk is that the executives struggle to formulate a common language. These different models elevate the experimentation activity to a higher level of visibility within the organization, making it more challenging for it to be killed off for its toxicity to the core.

It is critical that the *top management team engage with the experiment to provide the right level of ambition for the activity* (KSF#8). The flaw in the "minimal viable offer" approach is that it draws firms toward near-term product design issues. It is easier for teams tasked with leading such experiments to default to lower-risk activities that might result in short-term revenue rather than stretching for a larger opportunity that might involve longer development cycles. It is only the top management team that can ensure that the experiments focus remains firmly pegged to its disruptive ambitions.

Conclusion: Three Moments of Ambidexterity

Our research demonstrates the value of thinking about ambidexterity as having three distinct moments—ideation, incubation, and scaling—that share common features for success, such as the role of the senior team, and that also have distinct disciplines. Incubation is a frequent point of breakdown for firms that seek to build new businesses inside existing corporations; promising ideas simply don't progress. There are many useful lessons to learn from the start-up movement about how best to organize and execute new ventures as "business experiments." These lessons from the "start-up garage" enable established corporations to make progress on new ventures in a disciplined, fact-based way, while also moving at speed. We have identified eight key success factors for managing business experiments at the "incubation moment," which appear to improve the prospects of success.

Nevertheless, "acting like a start-up" is not enough to guarantee success. The organizational and culture inhibitors of success remain formidable, particularly when new ventures violate the rules of an existing core business. Getting started with ambidexterity involves actively managing these barriers from the start. The organizational and culture inhibitors of success remain formidable, particularly when new ventures violate the rules of an existing core business. We recommend that firms assess innovations for potential toxicity to the core so that they can take the appropriate steps to build capabilities or isolate the innovation organization needed to improve its prospects of success.

The engagement and behavior of the top management team remains critical to the success of ventures at each moment of ambidexterity. The capacity of these teams to engage with business experiments—even in a pre-revenue phase—is critical to overcoming the risks of "toxicity" and allowing a firm to learn about the potential areas for business growth.

Notes and References

1 The authors wish to acknowledge J. Andres Echeverry for his assistance in conducting research interviews for this study.

2 O'Reilly III, C. A. and M. L. Tushman. 2016. *Lead and disrupt: How to solve the innovator's dilemma*. Palo Alto, CA: Stanford University Press.

3 For example, Lawrence, P. R. and J. W. Lorsch. 1967. Differentiation and integration in complex organizations. *Administrative Science Quarterly* 12 (1); Donaldson, L. 2001. *The contingency theory of organizations*. Thousand Oaks, CA: Sage.

4 See Donaldson 2001; Tushman, M. L. and C. A. O'Reilly III 1997. *Winning through innovation*. Cambridge: Harvard Business School Press; O'Reilly and Tushman 2016.

5 O'Reilly and Tushman 2016.

6 Ibid.

7 O'Reilly III, C. A. and M. L. Tushman. 2013. Organizational ambidexterity: Past, present, and future. *Academy of Management Perspectives* 27 (4):324–38.

8 Our methodology for the research was 90-minute interviews with the corporate heads of innovation or strategy at the 26 companies using a structured questionnaire. This was mostly one interview per company. We started by inquiring into the innovation agenda for the firm and whether any exploratory business ventures had been launched. We then asked them to describe these exploratory business ventures in brief and, if possible, evaluate the success of the venture relative to expectations. All of the companies involved had launched at least one new business venture—there were a total of 35 new ventures across the 26 firms in the sample. We asked the interviewees to assess the success of the ventures relative to initial expectations. The interviewees coded nine as entirely or mostly successful and the rest as falling below expectations or as failures. In the interviewees, we asked subjects to describe how they managed several key issues identified in the literature as critical to setting up new business ventures. These included

- How did they make decisions about the appropriate strategy for the new business?
- How did they manage investments in the new business?
- In what ways was the new venture protected or incubated?
- What tools did they adopt in order to support the success of the new venture? (e.g., Stage-Gating, Design Thinking, Lean Start-Up)
- What specific organizational arrangements did they adopt to support the new venture, including management and decision-making systems?
- How was the leadership team involved in the new venture?

We pursued these questions with respect to each of the specific exploratory businesses identified by the interviewees. We sorted the data according to the success rating given to each of the exploratory ventures and sorted according to the different approaches adopted by the firms involved. Our findings are based on these data, together with our experience as practitioners supporting firms in making these decisions to establish ambidextrous units.

9 Kulash Jr., D. 2010. The new rock-star paradigm. *Wall Street Journal*, December 17.

10 *The Internet of things: Mapping the value beyond the hype*. 2015. Executive summary, McKinsey Global Institute, 55.

11 Blank, S. 2013. Why the lean start-up changes everything. *Harvard Business Review*, May.
12 Reis, E. 2011. *Lean start-up*. New York: Random House.
13 Kelley, T. 2001. *The art of innovation*. New York: Doubleday.
14 Binns, A., M. Tushman, and W. Smith. 2011. Ambidextrous CEO. *Harvard Business Review*, June.
15 Coley, S., M. Baghai, and D. White. 1999. *The alchemy of growth*. New York: Basic Books.
16 Slywotsky, A. J. 2002. *The profit zone*. New York: Three Rivers Press; Osterwalder, A. 2010. *Business model generation*, Hoboken, NJ: Wiley.
17 Binns, A., M. Tushman, C. O'Reilly, and B. Harreld. 2014. The art of strategic renewal. *Sloan Management Review*, Winter.
18 Groysberg, B. and L-E. Lee. 2009. Hiring stars and their colleagues: Exploration and exploitation in professional service firms, special issue on organizational ambidexterity. *Organization Science* 20 (4):740–58, June.

5 The MNC Matrix as Only a Partial Multiple Hierarchy
The Limited Advantage of the Matrix

Jane XJ Qiu and Lex Donaldson

Introduction

Conventionally scholars consider matrix structures more advantageous than simpler structures, because the matrix structures combine the information processing capacities of multiple hierarchies (Egelhoff 1991; Wolf and Egelhoff 2002). The present chapter probes this idea and suggests that matrix structures are not multiple hierarchies, as is often supposed. Consistent with this insight, matrix structures are found to have only a limited advantage over simpler structures in internationalization, the extent to which a firm depends on foreign markets for customers, the factors of production, and the capacity to create value (Sanders and Carpenter 1998). For multinational corporations (MNC), internationalization involves making sales in foreign countries, manufacturing in foreign countries, and transferring products between the parent country and foreign subsidiaries (Elango and Pattnaik 2007; Stopford and Wells 1972). In this chapter, we examine the view of a matrix being a multi-hierarchical structure and propose a new model to estimate the advantages possessed by matrix structures over simpler structures.

A matrix organizational structure is defined as any structure that employs a multiple command system in which employees report simultaneously to multiple bosses (Davis and Lawrence 1977; Ford and Randolph 1992; Galbraith 2009; Knight 1976). Matrix structures (e.g., a product-geographic matrix structure) are more complex than elementary structures (e.g., a geographical regions structure). Stopford and Wells (1972) and Franko (1976) provided early observations of matrix structures used by MNCs to control their foreign subsidiaries (hereinafter referred to as the "MNC matrix"). Among practitioners, the MNC matrix has received substantial interest (Galbraith 2009; Wolf and Egelhoff 2013), as evidenced by its use in large MNCs such as Proctor and Gamble (Piskorski and Spadini 2007), General Motors (Garvin and Levesque 2006), and IBM (Galbraith 2009).

Following its sometimes rather controversial popularity in the corporate world (Goggin 1974), the MNC matrix has attracted substantial research attention (Daniels, Pitts, and Tretter 1984, 1985; Davis and Lawrence 1977;

Donaldson 2009; Egelhoff 1991; Galbraith 2009; Galbraith and Kazanjian 1986; Kolodny 1981; Nohria and Ghoshal 1997; Stopford and Wells 1972; Wolf and Egelhoff 2002). The majority of the studies of the MNC matrix suggest that they are more advantageous than elementary structures in attaining higher degrees of internationalization because the matrix combines multiple elementary structures into a multi-hierarchical structure (Chi and Nystrom 1998; Goggin 1974; Morschett, Schramm-Klein, and Zentes 2010; Segal-Horn and Faulkner 2010). Each elementary structure in the matrix is considered to be a hierarchy that processes information for the MNC (Egelhoff 1988a; Wolf and Egelhoff 2002; Wolf, Egelhoff, and Adzic 2007). The idea of the MNC matrix as being multi-hierarchical and combining the information processing capacities of the elementary structures that compose it is quite widely accepted in the literature (Galbraith 2009; Larson and Gobeli 1987). However, little work has been done to clarify the extent to which the matrix structure is actually multi-hierarchical and thereby ascertaining the extent to which a matrix structure is able to provide the combined information processing capacities of the elementary structures that comprise it.

Further, although it is widely understood that the MNC matrix provides the advantage to pursue simultaneously dual international strategies, such as geographic diversification and corporate integration (Daniels, Pitts, and Tretter 1984, 1985; Qiu and Donaldson 2012; Stopford and Wells 1972), little has been done to understand to what extent a matrix actually helps to attain higher degrees of internationalization for MNCs. Understanding the amount of benefit and advantage of such a structure is important to decision makers because restructuring an organization into a matrix structure is costly and carries the potential risk of problems such as role conflict and power struggles (Barker, Tjosvold, and Andrews 1988; Larson and Gobeli 1987). Managers must balance the advantage delivered by a matrix structure against the cost. Therefore, the issue of how much advantage a matrix really confers on an MNC becomes salient for managers, consultants, and business school academics.

Motivated by these gaps in the literature and practitioner interest, we seek to advance research on the MNC matrix and its advantage. Specifically, we seek to explore the matrix advantage by trying to answer two questions: (1) Do matrices have an advantage over elementary structures in attaining internationalization? (2) If yes, can we model the matrix advantage to understand the extent to which matrices are more advantageous than elementary structures in facilitating internationalization? We first examine the conventional assumption that an MNC matrix contains multiple hierarchies and then propose the contrasting view that an MNC matrix generally only contains a single hierarchy. The two different ideas have different implications for the information processing capacity that a matrix structure confers on an MNC and thus the degrees of internationalization that are attained by an MNC matrix structure. We calculate the difference in the degrees of internationalization that are attained for an MNC by a matrix as compared with an elementary structure. In this way, we critically assess the supposed advantage of matrix structures in facilitating internationalization.

This chapter makes two contributions to the literature. It critiques the widely accepted idea that an MNC matrix is multi-hierarchical and thus substantially more advantageous than elementary structures. Second, this study provides a quantitative estimate of the extent to which an MNC matrix delivers higher internationalization, which is in line with the calls for theoretical and empirical eclecticism in international business studies (Cheng, Henisz, Roth, and Swaminathan 2009; Shapira 2011). This study is exploratory in its nature, but, hopefully, it will help advance the literature on MNC organizational design.

A Critique of the Matrix as a Multi-hierarchical Structure

By extending the strategy-structure tradition of Chandler (1962) to MNCs, the seminal studies of Stopford and Wells (1972) and Franko (1976) marked the beginnings of international strategy-structure research (Burton, Obel, and Håkonsson 2015; Daniels, Pitts, and Tretter 1984, 1985; Davis and Lawrence 1977; Donaldson 2009; Egelhoff 1991; Stopford and Wells 1972; Wolf and Egelhoff 2002). Following this research tradition, we focus on the macro structure through which a headquarters (HQ) seeks to control its subsidiaries. For brevity and simplicity, we will focus on the two-dimensional matrix rather than the three- or four-dimensional matrices, though the argument also applies to them.

It has been widely accepted that the MNC matrix, in comparison with elementary global structures, possesses extra advantages by having multiple hierarchies (Galbraith 2009; Larson and Gobeli 1987; Stopford and Wells 1972). For example, managers are cautioned about the need to maintain "two separate hierarchies" if they choose a matrix structure (Wolf and Egelhoff 2002, 183). Few scholars, however, have carefully examined the details of this idea, which is often taken for granted in theoretical reasoning about the MNC matrix. We suggest that, on the contrary, matrix structures typically possess only a single hierarchy.

To scrutinize the assumption of the MNC matrix being multi-hierarchical, we start by exploring its graphical representation, which is frequently used to illustrate the difference between various MNC structures (Jones 2001; Morschett et al. 2010). This representation tends to give a false impression that matrix structures have multiple hierarchies. Figures 5.1a and 5.1b illustrate the typical graphical representation in textbooks to illustrate a matrix (e.g., Jones 2001, 162, 172, 184; Morschett et al. 2010, 184, 185, 189) using the examples of an elementary geographic division structure and a product-geographic matrix. Whereas an MNC using an elementary structure, such as, for instance, a geographical-regions structure, has the regional heads under the CEO, the MNC using a matrix structure has two sets of senior executives under the CEO: the regional heads and the product heads.

The graphical representation in Figure 5.1b highlights the matrix characteristic as multidimensional rather than a single dimension of an elementary structure (as in Figure 5.1a). However, only part of the whole organizational hierarchy is visualized in Figure 5.1b. In the international strategy-structure literature, the multi-boss matrix usually exists in the interface between the HQ and the foreign subsidiaries (Davis and Lawrence 1977; Egelhoff 1982; Stopford and Wells 1972). Below the managers with two bosses (i.e., the two-boss managers), the majority of personnel in the MNC are still organized in a one-boss hierarchy (Davis and Lawrence 1977; Galbraith 2002). For example, the head of a foreign subsidiary in Region C manufacturing Product C reports to both the manager of Region C and the manager of

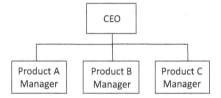

Figure 5.1a Typical representation of an MNC using an elementary structure

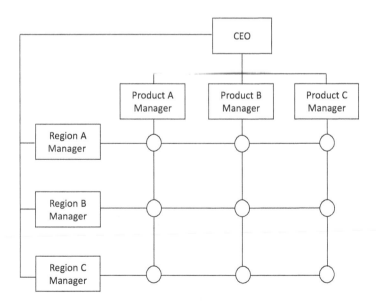

Figure 5.1b Typical representation of an MNC using a matrix structure

Product C in the HQ. Reporting to the head of this subsidiary are the senior managers within the subsidiary. However, these subsidiary managers and their subordinates may be in a single chain of command of hierarchical levels that stretch down to the shop floor so that there is a single hierarchy under the subsidiary head. Nevertheless, as can be seen in Figure 5.1b, the hierarchical levels below the two-boss managers (i.e., the subsidiary heads) are often omitted in the graphical representation of an MNC using a matrix structure. Hence this widely used graphical representation of a matrix structure illustrated in Figure 5.1b is incomplete because it fails to show all the hierarchy and so is somewhat misleading.

In contrast, a more adequate representation of a matrix would show the complete organizational hierarchy of an MNC matrix, as in Figure 5.2b. This is similar to the singular hierarchy of an elementary structure (as shown in Figure 5.2a)—apart from a single level. In the product-geographical matrix, for example, three levels of personnel are directly related to the multiple command system: (1) the CEO (the top leadership), to whom the HQ senior managers report; (2) the HQ senior managers (the matrix bosses); and (3) the matrix managers, each of whom is controlled by two different senior managers simultaneously. The multidimensional feature exists only on the second hierarchical level. Here coexist two structural dimensions: the worldwide product structural dimension and the geographical regions' structural dimension (in the case of the product-geographical type of matrix). Hence information is being processed simultaneously by two sets of specialists in the HQ: a set of product specialists (e.g., manager of Product C in the worldwide product structural dimension) and a set of regional specialists (e.g., manager of Region C in the geographical regions' structural dimension). Under these senior managers (i.e., the matrix bosses) are the matrix managers (i.e., the two-boss managers). These managers are reporting simultaneously to these two lines of senior managers above them.

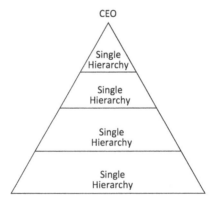

Figure 5.2a The hierarchy of an MNC using an elementary structure

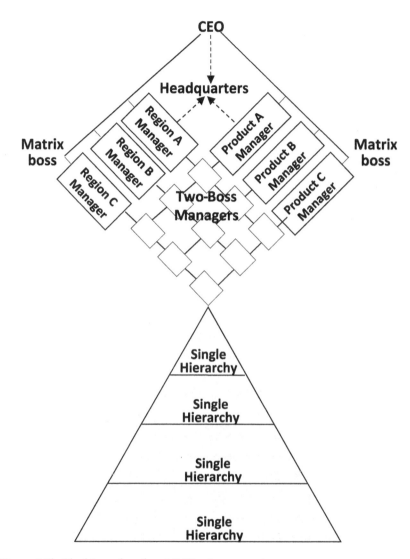

Figure 5.2b The hierarchy of an MNC using a matrix structure

However, below these two-boss managers, the employees have only one boss directly in charge of them (Davis and Lawrence 1977; Galbraith 2002). Below the two-boss managers, the managers and other employees are usually organized in a single hierarchy.

There may be exceptions, but they do not overturn the main point that in a matrix, the multidimensional structure may exist at only a single level. Some matrices may exist at lower hierarchical levels (e.g., in a research lab) in some organizations. In an organization, matrices can exist simultaneously at more than one hierarchical level. But the existence of a matrix at a high hierarchical level does not mean that there will necessarily also be a matrix lower down. Thus high-level matrix structures of the kind featured in MNCs can coexist with there being a single hierarchy at middle and lower levels of the organizational hierarchy. Generally, a high-level matrix structure in an organization can coexist with a single hierarchy below it.

We argue that when an MNC uses a matrix, the multiple structural dimensions often exist only partially on one hierarchical level in the whole MNC. They exist on the level under the CEO, but above the rest of the MNC structure. Other than this level, the rest of the structure will tend to be mainly still one single command system and thus still be organized in one single-structural dimension with a single hierarchy, as illustrated in Figure 5.2b. Thus the organization, despite being a matrix at the high level, is not a multiple hierarchy. The matrix is compatible with the organizational personnel mainly being in a single hierarchy, with the two-boss managers in the matrix being the exception.

It is tempting to speak of matrix structures as being combinations of two elementary structures, such as "geographic divisions" and "product divisions," but this is erroneous. Matrix structures may be correctly said to comprise two structural dimensions, such as geography and product, for example. However, the matrix does not thereby comprise all the features of those elementary structures. The matrix structure does not have all the personnel at the various hierarchical levels that a geographical-regions structure and a product-divisions structure, for instance, would have. More specifically, the matrix structure does not have two hierarchies. While the two types of specialization, e.g., product and geography, are present in the matrix organization, *both* the complete geographic and complete product organizations are *not* present. In that sense, it is misleading to speak of a matrix structure as comprising two elementary structures (Galbraith 2009; Jones 2001; Larson and Gobeli 1987; Morschett et al. 2010; Stopford and Wells 1972; Wolf and Egelhoff 2002) because they do not comprise all the features of the elementary structures. In particular, they do not have the two hierarchies that the two elementary structures possess.

Information Processing in Matrix Structures

The earlier discussion sought to clarify the concept of the MNC matrix structure by questioning the number of levels in the organizational hierarchy of the multidimensional structure. We have proposed that in the majority of MNCs using a matrix structure, the multiple structural dimensions exist only at one level. Hence two contrasting views can be empirically tested and compared to advance our understanding of the MNC matrix. The first view is based on the conventional assumption that the MNC matrix is multi-hierarchical (combining multiple "elementary structures"). The second view is based on our proposition that, in general, MNCs using a matrix are still mainly a single hierarchy, only partially combining multiple structural dimensions at one hierarchical level.

These two different structural views have different implications for the MNCs' pursuit of internationalization. These can be explained by the information processing perspective, which is widely used in the international strategy-structure tradition to conceptualize the relationship between strategy and structure (Egelhoff 1982, 1988a, 1988b, 1991; Galbraith 2009; Qiu and Donaldson 2010, 2012; Wolf and Egelhoff 2002; Wolf et al. 2007). From this perspective, MNCs have strategy-structure fits when the information processing capacities of their structures fit the information processing requirements of their strategies (Egelhoff 1982). Matrices can be viewed as the "overlaying" of multiple elementary structures (Egelhoff 1988a, 3; Wolf et al. 2007, 4), and each of the elementary structures combined in the matrix exists as a structural dimension that processes information for the MNC (Egelhoff 1988a, 1988b; Galbraith 2009).

Thus the MNC matrix is conceived of as a structure that combines "in an additive manner the individual information processing capacities of the elementary structural dimensions that comprise the matrix" (Wolf and Egelhoff 2002, 182). And "the information processing capacity of a matrix can be viewed as the addition or sum of the information processing capacities of its dimensions" (Wolf et al. 2007, 8). Furthermore,

> the view that a matrix structure provides not just multiple dimensions of information processing within an organization, but, more specifically, the information processing capacities of the two or three elementary dimensions represented in the matrix is potentially a powerful idea.
> (Wolf and Egelhoff 2002, 182)

The information processing perspective views a matrix as a multidimensional information processing system (Galbraith 2009) and thus enables an organization to process more information that is related to a certain strategy (Egelhoff 1988a, 1988b; Wolf and Egelhoff 2002; Wolf et al. 2007). When a structure provides a high degree of capacity to process information that is relevant to a strategy, it facilitates a high degree of the strategic activity required by that strategy and thus fits a high degree of that particular strategy (Donaldson 2009; Egelhoff 1988a, 1988b). If the information processing capacities of the elementary structural dimensions in a matrix can be added together to form a higher information processing capacity of the matrix, MNCs using a matrix should have a higher degree of that particular strategy than those using only one of the elementary structures. The advantage in information processing from a matrix structure shows itself in the enhanced degree of internationalization and thereby attainment of MNC goals.

In the literature, the use of an MNC matrix is associated with a high degree of internationalization. Effective organizational structures for the

MNC would help produce higher sales and manufacturing in foreign countries, which capture a firm's degree of internationalization, thereby attaining location-specific advantages (Qian and Li 1998; Wiersema and Bowen 2008). As the degree of foreign sales and manufacturing increases, an MNC needs to handle a larger amount of information to deal with different business environments in various geographic areas. Also, effective organizational structures for the MNC would help produce higher degrees of transfer of products between foreign and domestic businesses to yield economies of scale. Such corporate integration represents the coordination of activities within an MNC on a global scale (Dunning and Robson 1987), such as global sourcing or centralized production in a low-cost country. A high degree of corporate integration leads to increased interdependence within the MNC, thereby requiring increased coordination between the subunits (Cheng 1983; Roth, Schweiger, and Morrison 1991). To facilitate such coordination, an MNC needs to process a large amount of information between HQ and the subsidiary, as well as between different subsidiaries. Thus more effective organizational structures will provide more information processing that will lead to the attainment of internationalization by the MNC. From the viewpoint of matrix structures having multiple structural dimensions as information processing channels, matrix structures would be expected to provide greater information processing capacity than elementary structures. Therefore, matrix structures are more effective when it comes to high degrees of internationalization in comparison with single-dimensional elementary structures that make less provision for the complexity and coordination challenges required by high degrees of internationalization. We expect the matrix advantage in MNCs to manifest itself by higher degrees of internationalization in MNCs with matrix structures than in MNCs with only elementary structures.

MNC Matrix Study

Wolf and Egelhoff (2002) made important contributions to international strategy-structure theory by showing the strategy-structure fits of various structural dimensions contained in both elementary structures and matrices. The strategy scores of different structures were added together; however, their method of analysis was to compare groupings of structures that contain *both* elementary and matrix structures (e.g., "GR + FD x GR" Geographical Regions' elementary structure plus Functional Divisions-Geographical Regions' matrix structure, Wolf and Egelhoff (2002, table 2, 186). This means that any effects of the matrices were mixed in with those of the elementary structures (Wolf et al. 2007). Hence their analysis did not address the question pursued here about whether the matrix has any advantage over the elementary structures. The mean levels of internationalization of the MNCs using each structure were published by Wolf and Egelhoff (2002) and provide the data used in our secondary analysis.

The study of Wolf and Egelhoff (2002) measured three variables that capture various aspects of internationalization: foreign sales, foreign manufacturing, and intracompany transfers. These three variables together capture internationalization in a comprehensive manner, and we use them in our secondary analysis in the next section.

Foreign sales termed "size of foreign operation" by Wolf and Egelhoff (2002) were measured by "the percentage of a company's sales occurring outside of the parent country" (Wolf and Egelhoff 2002, 189). Conceptually, the foreign sales variable measures the "foreignness" of sales. It reflects the weight and importance of the foreign market(s) in a firm's operation. For foreign sales to be high, a firm has to process more information to coordinate activities within and between various geographic locations. For each type of structure, Wolf and Egelhoff give the mean percentage of their sales that are foreign. For convenience, this is re-expressed here as the ratio of the foreign sales of a firm to its total sales.

Foreign manufacturing, termed "size of foreign manufacturing" by Wolf and Egelhoff (2002), was measured by "the percentage of a company's manufacturing occurring outside of the parent country" (Wolf and Egelhoff 2002, 189). Conceptually, the foreign manufacturing variable measures the foreignness of production activities. It is also closely associated with geographic diversification, and in particular it reflects the depth of a firm's geographic expansion. For foreign manufacturing to be high, a firm has to process more information to coordinate production activities within and between various geographic locations. For each structure, Wolf and Egelhoff give the mean percentage of their manufacturing that is foreign. This is re-expressed here as the ratio of foreign manufacturing to total manufacturing.

Intracompany transfers were measured by "adding (1) the percentage of the parent company's procurement of final and intermediate products that are sourced from the company's foreign operations, and (2) the percentage of the parent company's sales which are transfers to the company's foreign operations" (Wolf and Egelhoff 2002, 189). Conceptually, the intracompany transfers' variable measures the foreignness of parental procurement and of parental sales (rather than company sales). It captures the need for coordination between HQ and foreign subsidiaries and also the intensity of corporate integration (Donaldson 2009; Qiu and Donaldson 2012). For each structure, Wolf and Egelhoff give the mean percentage of their intracompany transfers that are foreign. This is re-expressed here as the ratios of foreign parental procurement to total parental procurement and of foreign company sales to company sales added together. The three variables, foreign sales, foreign manufacturing, and intracompany transfers, in the study of Wolf and Egelhoff (2002) all tap aspects of the foreignness of MNC operations. All these foreignness variables were positively intercorrelated between 0.32 and 0.51 (with an average of 0.43), which is consistent with their measuring various aspects of a singular construct, i.e., internationalization. The measurement of this construct is, however, not exhaustive in that other aspects of internationalization may well exist. Nevertheless, the present analysis of internationalization is quite informative, covering as it does sales, manufacturing, and product transfers. The three variables "hang together" and so collectively shed light on the degree of internationalization of an MNC.

Ten different types of structure were identified in Wolf and Egelhoff's (2002) study. Because our focus is the matrix and its constituent elementary structures, we analyzed only the three (two-dimensional) matrices and the three elementary structures that are said by Wolf and Egelhoff to comprise these matrices. For example, the functional-geographic matrix consists (according to Wolf and Egelhoff 2002, table 2, 186) of the worldwide functional divisions' elementary structure and the worldwide geographical regions' elementary structure. The three elementary structures used in the present analysis were the worldwide functional divisions, the worldwide geographical regions, and the worldwide product divisions. The three matrices were the functional-geographic matrix, the product-functional matrix, and the product-geographic matrix.

For each structural type, e.g., worldwide functional divisions, its mean level on each of the three internationalization variables is given in Table 5.1. For example, for the firms with a worldwide functional-divisions structure, the ratio of foreign sales to total sales was 0.42, which means, for a firm with a worldwide functional-divisions structure, on average 42% of its sales occur outside of the parent country. Because the empirical section of this chapter is a secondary analysis of the results published in Wolf and Egelhoff (2002), the figure of 0.42 is adopted from Wolf and Egelhoff (2002, 186, table 2), as are the figures for all the other structural types (which are shown in the first six columns of Table 5.1).

Returning to the example of the worldwide functional divisions, the score of 0.42 for foreign sales has the following meaning. For each firm, their sales from foreign countries were expressed as a percentage of their total sales. The percentages were then averaged across the firms with the same type of structure. For instance, for the firms with the worldwide functional-divisions structure, their mean foreign sales were 42%. In the present analysis, this percentage figure was re-expressed as a ratio, 0.42, i.e., the ratio of foreign sales to total sales was 0.42. Similarly, for the firms with the product-functional matrix structure, their mean foreign sales ratio was 0.55.

These ratios are comparable. For example, the mean of 0.42 for the foreign sales for firms with the worldwide functional-divisions structure can be compared with the figure of 0.55 for the foreign sales of the firms with the product-functional matrix structure. This indicates that the degree of foreignness of sales is higher for firms with the product-functional matrix structure than for those firms with a worldwide functional-divisions structure. The product-functional matrix structure has an advantage over the simpler structure of the worldwide functional divisions. The product-functional matrix structure is more conducive to garnering higher sales from foreign

Table 5.1 The Internationalization of Structures in MNCs

Internationalization	Functional divisions	Geographic regions	Product divisions	Total elementary structures	Functional-geographic matrix	Product-functional matrix	Product-geographic matrix	Total matrix structures
Number of MNCs	8	2	19	29	5	6	5	16
Foreign sales	0.42	0.58	0.56	1.56	0.59	0.55	0.67	1.81
Foreign manufacturing	0.28	0.40	0.34	1.02	0.47	0.43	0.38	1.28
Intracompany transfers	0.42	0.06	0.28	0.76	0.38	0.28	0.40	1.06

countries than the worldwide functional-divisions structure. Thereby, on the foreign sales aspect of internationalization, the product-functional matrix has an advantage over the worldwide functional-divisions structure.

Next, we address two questions: (1) Is there an advantage of matrices over elementary structures in attaining internationalization? (2) If yes, can we model the matrix advantage of the degree to which matrices have an advantage over elementary structures in internationalization? As we will explain in the following section, the fully additive model and the partially additive model are used to try to predict the matrix advantage in attaining a higher degree of foreign sales, foreign manufacturing, and intracompany transfers.

Quantifying the Advantage of the Matrix

Now we quantify the matrix advantage. As we have argued, the issue is to address the additional information processing capacity that comes from combining matrix structures in the additive manner used by Wolf and Egelhoff. As just seen, the foreign sales ratio of the functional elementary structure was 0.42 (see Table 5.1) and that of the geographical-regions elementary structure was 0.58. Furthermore, that of the product-divisions elementary structure was 0.56. Therefore, the total foreign sales ratio available from these three elementary structures was 0.42 + 0.58 + 0.56—that is, 1.56. In comparison, the foreign sales ratio of the functional-geographic matrix structure was 0.59, that of the product-functional matrix structure was 0.55, and that of the product-geographic matrix structure was 0.67 (Table 5.1). Therefore, the total foreign sales ratio of the matrices was 0.59 + 0.55 + 0.67, and the sum is 1.81. The advantage of the matrix structures is 1.81 less the 1.56 of the elementary structures, so it is 0.25 (= 1.81–1.56). This is only 16% (= 0.25/1.56 x 100) of the elementary structure. Thus a matrix advantage existed, but is only limited.

Similarly, the foreign manufacturing ratio of the functional elementary structure was 0.28, which means a firm with a functional structure on average has 28% of its manufacturing activities occurring outside of the parent country. The foreign manufacturing ratio of the geographical regions' elementary structure was 0.40 and that of the product-divisions elementary structure was 0.34 (Table 5.1). Therefore, the total foreign manufacturing of these elementary structures was 0.28 + 0.40 + 0.34, which is 1.02. In comparison, the foreign manufacturing ratio of the functional-geographic matrix structure was 0.47, that of the product-functional matrix structure was 0.43, and that of the product-geographic matrix structure was 0.38 (Table 5.1). Therefore, the total foreign manufacturing ratio of the matrices was 0.47 + 0.43 + 0.38, which is 1.28. The advantage of the matrix structures was 0.26 (= 1.28 – 1.02). This is 25%. Again, an advantage existed for the matrices over the elementary structures, but it is only limited.

Similarly, again, the total intracompany transfers ratio of the three elementary structures (Table 5.1) was 0.42 + 0.06 + 0.28—that is, 0.76. In comparison, the total of the three matrices was 0.38 + 0.28 + 0.40—that is, 1.06. Thus the advantage of the matrix structures was 0.30 (= 1.06 – 0.76). This is 39%. Once again, the matrix advantage existed, but is only limited.

In summary, the matrix advantage was only limited for these three internationalization variables: 16% for foreign sales, 25% for foreign manufacturing, and 39% for intracompany transfers. For all these aspects of internationalization, the matrix advantage was much less than the 100% that it would be if creating a matrix structure meant doubling the information processing capability by adding a second elementary structure to the first elementary structure. Hence the answer to our first question is matrices do have an advantage over elementary structures in attaining internationalization; however, the extent of this advantage is only limited.

The second question is answered in the following section by developing models of the matrix advantage, so as to better understand why matrices are more advantageous than elementary structures in facilitating internationalization. We developed two, contrasting models to quantify how much higher the degrees of internationalization attained by matrices are—that is, the amount of the matrix advantage in comparison to the elementary structures. The first model is named the fully additive model, and the second is named the partially additive model, as explained in the next section. We find that the fully additive model is empirically invalid, whereas the partially additive model is empirically valid.

The Fully Additive Model and Its Invalidity

The fully additive model is based on the view that a matrix, as the combination of multiple elementary structures, contains multiple hierarchies. For instance, in a geographic-product matrix, there are hierarchies both from the heads of the geographies down to the shop floor and also from the heads of the products down to the shop floor. Thus a matrix is considerably more advantageous than an elementary structure as a result of combining the full amount of information processing capacities of the multiple hierarchies of its supposedly constituent elementary structures. Consequently, the fully additive model postulates that the matrix fully combines the information processing capacities of its (supposedly) constituent elementary structures to attain a high degree of internationalization.

For example, in a geographic-product matrix, the degree of the internationalization of the geographical-regions elementary structure is added to the degree of the internationalization of the product-divisions elementary structure to give the expected degree of internationalization of the geographic-product matrix. The logic is that if the matrix combines two elementary structures, it should possess the information processing of both of them. Therefore, the second structural dimension of the matrix should add 100% of its internationalization to that of the first structural dimension.

The fully additive model, derived from the view of the matrix as a multiple hierarchy, predicts the internationalization degree attained by a matrix to be the sum of the internationalization degrees of both its elementary structures. For instance, consider the degree of foreign sales. In Table 5.1, we see that, for the worldwide functional division, its foreign sales ratio was 0.42. In the next column of Table 5.1, we see that, for the worldwide geographic structure, its foreign sales ratio was 0.58. Thus when these two elementary structures are combined by being in a functional-geographic matrix, the foreign sales of the functional-geographic matrix would be predicted to be 0.42 + 0.58—that is, 1.00 according to the fully additive model. Thus the foreign sales ratio of the MNCs with a functional-geographic matrix would be expected to be 1.00. However, the actual foreign sales of the functional-geographic matrix were only .59.

Thus the actual foreign sales ratio attained by MNCs with the functional-geographic matrix (0.59) was much less than that which would be predicted from the model that the contributions of their two constituent structures would fully add together to give 1.00. The prediction error of the fully additive model was 0.41. Therefore, the fully additive model prediction exceeds the actual foreign sales by 69% (i.e., 0.41/0.59 x 100%). The fully additive model does not give a valid prediction of the foreign sales of the functional-geographic matrix. These results challenge the presumption that the functional-geographic matrix fully combines the degrees of attainments of the functional and geographic structures because the matrix gives the information processing capacity from two hierarchies.

For both the product-functional matrix and the product-geographic matrix, we find that their actual degrees of foreign sales were, again, much less than are predicted by the fully additive models. The foreign sales ratio for the product-functional matrix was predicted to be 0.98 (i.e., 0.56 + 0.42, in Table 5.1), yet in actuality they were only 0.55, an error of 0.43—that is, 78%. And the foreign sales ratio for the product-geographic matrix was predicted to be 1.14 (i.e., 0.56 + 0.58, in table 5.1), yet was only 0.67, an error of 0.47—that is, 70%.

In total, the predicted foreign sales ratio for the three matrices (functional-geographic matrix, product-functional matrix, and product-geographic matrix) was 3.12 (i.e., 1.00 + 0.98 + 1.14). In contrast, the total actual foreign sales ratio for these three matrices was 1.81 (i.e., 0.59 + 0.55 + 0.67, see Table 5.2). The prediction of the foreign sales ratio by the fully additive model exceeded the actual degree (3.12 − 1.81)/1.81 x 100% by 72% (of the actual degree). This means that the fully additive model can be considered to have an error of 72% (Table 5.2).

As we can see in Table 5.2 (third column), the predictions by the fully additive model for the matrices exceeded the actual degrees of the internationalization variables substantially: 72% for foreign sales, 59% for foreign

Table 5.2 Errors of Fully versus Partially Additive Models of Matrices

Internationalization	Matrix: Actual	Matrix: Fully additive predictions	Matrix: Fully additive errors	Matrix: Partially additive predictions	Matrix: Partially additive errors
Foreign sales	1.81	3.12	72%	1.92	6%
Foreign manufacturing	1.28	2.04	59%	1.27	–1%
Intracompany transfers	1.06	1.52	43%	1.18	11%

manufacturing, and 43% for intracompany transfers. For all three internationalization variables, the fully additive model led to predictions that were substantially greater than the actual degrees. The actual degrees of internationalization of the matrices were much smaller than the sums of the internationalization of the elementary structures that may be thought to comprise them. The fully additive model considerably overestimates the extra advantage provided by the matrix relative to the elementary structure in attaining a higher degree of internationalization. The advantage of the matrix was only modest and was consistent with the matrix possessing much less information processing capacity than is postulated by the fully additive model.

The Partially Additive Model and Its Validity

The partially additive model is based on the view of the matrix as being multiple structural dimensions at only a single hierarchical degree out of the whole MNC hierarchy. Instead of being thoroughly multidimensional, an MNC using a matrix is still mainly single dimensional throughout the organization. Accordingly, the partial multidimensional structure adds information processing capacity proportionately to the matrix level existing at only one of the many hierarchical levels in the organization.

To develop the idea of "partially additive" into a quantitative model, we need to think at a conceptual level about the way in which the multiple structural dimensions are combined in a matrix. In contingency theory, which is the theoretical foundation of the strategy-structure paradigm (Donaldson 2001), the structure that best fits a strategy will produce the highest degree of that strategy in comparison to other structures available and such a structure is usually considered as the best-fitting structure for that strategy. For example, the product-divisions structure is the best-fitting structure for the product diversity strategy and empirically has been found to have the highest degree of product diversification among various structures (Chandler 1962; Stopford and Wells 1972).

To construct the model, we postulate that the structural dimension in a matrix that best fits internationalization is the elementary structural dimension with the highest individual degree of internationalization. The best-fitting elementary structural dimension is considered to be the primary structural dimension in the matrix, and it serves as the main hierarchy for information processing activities. The other elementary structural dimension is secondary and adds extra information processing capacity to attain a higher degree of internationalization for the MNC by combining with the best-fitting structural dimension. (It should be noted that nominating the best-fitting elementary structure as the primary structural dimension in the matrix produces a somewhat higher internationalization degree for the matrix than would nominating the second best-fitting elementary structure. Therefore, it is a conservative assumption relative to the overall argument of this chapter that the matrix has only a modest advantage over elementary structures.)

We postulate that the best-fitting elementary structural dimension acts as the main hierarchy in the matrix and contributes the full amount (100%) of its information processing capacity. In contrast, the secondary elementary structural dimension adds to only one of the MNC's hierarchical levels to form the matrix structure. The strategy degree of the best-fitting elementary structural dimension is combined with only one part of the secondary elementary structural dimension to form the multidimensional structure. The secondary structural dimension in the matrix contributes its information processing capacity proportionately to the matrix being only one of the many hierarchical levels of the MNC. Hence the secondary structural dimension in the matrix is giving only $1/h$ (where h is the number of hierarchical levels in the MNC) of its individual information processing capacity to the matrix.

Consistent with how information processing capacities of its elementary structures are combined in only one level of the organizational hierarchy, the partially additive model posits that a matrix attains a higher degree of internationalization than the best-fitting elementary structure by a proportion of $1/h$ of the degree of internationalization attained by the secondary elementary structures. Thus the internationalization degree of the matrix in the partially additive model is the result of the full internationalization of the best-fitting elementary structure plus a fraction ($1/h$) of the internationalization attained by the secondary elementary structure.

One issue in applying the partially additive model is to know the average number of hierarchical levels (i.e., h) of the MNCs in Wolf and Egelhoff's (2002) study. This number was not given in Wolf and Egelhoff's (2002) data, but it can be estimated using two pieces of information: the number of employees and the span of control (Abdel-Khalik 1988). In Wolf and Egelhoff's (2002) study, the average number of employees of the German MNCs was 24,419. Although the span of control varies in different organizations, we used the approximation of the average span of control in an average company, as the goal of this chapter is to advance a general theory about the best available estimate of matrix advantage. The average span of control of an organization can be obtained from the data of Blau and Schoenherr (1971) and, on average across a large number of organizations, is about six. A more recent report on workforce management has found that the average span of control in companies across different industries approximates seven (Davison 2003).

In a pyramidal hierarchy, where the number of employees is 24,419, using either six or seven as the span of control results in a number of hierarchical levels (*h*) of seven by the formula in Abdel-Khalik (1988). Hence an estimate of seven as the average number of hierarchical levels (*h*) of the firms studied by Wolf and Egelhoff (2002) is used in the partially additive model. Thus the secondary elementary structural dimension adds only one-seventh (1/7)—that is, 14%—of its information processing capacity to a matrix. Therefore, the prediction by the partially additive model of the internationalization degree for the matrices is the sum of the full amount of the internationalization degree of the best-fitting elementary structural dimension and 14% of the internationalization degree of the secondary structural dimension.

Considering the functional-geographic matrix, the foreign sales ratio of the geographical-regions structure was 0.58, which was higher than the foreign sales of the functional division at 0.42 (Table 5.1). Therefore, the best-fitting elementary structural dimension was the geographical-regions structure, and its foreign sales ratio was 0.58. The secondary structural dimension was the functional division, and its foreign sales ratio was 0.42, 14% of which was 0.06. Therefore, the predicted foreign sales ratio for the functional-geographic matrix was 0.64 (i.e., 0.58 + 0.06). This was higher than the actual foreign sales of the functional-geographic matrix at 0.59 (Table 5.1), but only by 0.05. That was an error of only 8% (of the actual foreign sales).

Similarly, for the product-functional matrix, the best-fitting elementary structural dimension was the product-divisions structure in which the foreign sales ratio was 0.56 (Table 5.1). This was higher than the foreign sales of the functional division, 0.42, of which 14% was 0.06. Therefore, the predicted foreign sales ratio for the product-functional matrix was 0.62 (i.e., 0.56 + 0.06). The actual foreign sales of the product-functional matrix were 0.55, so the prediction by the partially additive model (0.62) exceeded the actual by 7, an error of only 13%.

Similarly, again, for the product-geographic matrix, the best-fitting elementary structural dimension was the geographical regions, whose foreign sales ratio was 0.58 (Table 5.1). This was higher than the foreign sales ratio of the product-divisions structure at 0.56, of which 14% was 0.08. Therefore, the predicted foreign sales ratio for the product-geographic matrix was 0.66 (i.e., 0.58 + 0.08). The actual foreign sales ratio of the product-functional matrix was 0.67, so the prediction by the partially additive model (0.66) understates the actual foreign sales by 1, an error of only 1%.

As just seen, for the three matrices, their predicted foreign sales by the partially additive model were 0.64 + 0.62 + 0.66, which in aggregate is a total of 1.92 (Table 5.2). Their actual total sales were 1.81 (i.e., 0.59 + 0.55 + 0.67). This was a difference of only 11. The partially additive model overstates the foreign sales of the matrices by only 6% (of actual foreign sales, i.e., (192 − 181)/181). This is far less than the fully additive model that overstates foreign sales of the matrices by 72% (as seen earlier). Thus, for foreign sales, the partially additive model had superior predictive power as compared with the fully additive model.

By the same partially additive method, the results were calculated for the foreign manufacturing and the intracompany transfers variables. Table 5.2 shows that the predictions by the partially additive model for the matrices deviated only slightly from the actual degrees: 6% (of the actual degree) for foreign sales, −1% for foreign manufacturing, and 11% for intracompany transfers. Moreover, while the partially additive model results exceeded the actual results for foreign sales and intracompany transfers, for foreign manufacturing, the partially additive result is slightly *less* than the actual. Thus, across the three internationalization variables, the results for the partially additive model are straddling the actual values, indicating that the partially additive model was a working approximation of the relationship between matrix structures and internationalization.

The accuracy of the partially additive model was high and higher than that of the fully additive model. For foreign sales, the error of the fully additive model was 72%, whereas the error for the partially additive model was only 6%. Similarly, for foreign manufacturing, the error of the fully additive model was 59%, whereas the error for the partially additive model was only (minus) 1%. And again, for intracompany transfers, the error of the fully additive model was 43%, whereas the error for the partially additive model was only 11%. The partially additive model was more accurate than the fully additive model in predicting the degree of internationalization attained by the matrix structure.

In summary, the matrix advantage existed but was only limited for the three internationalization variables at between 16% and 39%. And the partially additive model explained this with an error of only between −1% and 11%.

The results herein are consistent with the partially additive model enjoying more validity than the fully additive model. This in turn signifies that there is only a modest advantage in information processing of the matrix structure over the elementary structure. This again is compatible with the structural dimensions of a matrix not being multiple elementary structures. Accordingly, a matrix structure is mainly a single hierarchy, with multiple command structures limited to a single level in the hierarchy. While the analysis in this chapter has been of MNCs, their type of high-level matrix structure is not confined to MNCs and may be found in other corporations so that the analysis potentially generalizes to them.

This study has a number of limitations, including (1) using secondary analysis instead of self-collected data that more accurately captures the variable being studied; (2) the data used included only German manufacturing firms (Wolf and Egelhoff 2002), which is a limited representation of MNCs; and (3) internationalization is captured by variables that measure the degree of internationalization of manufacturing MNCs, but the degree of internationalization of service MNCs may be quite different. A welcome development in future studies would be to study performance as the outcome variable, perhaps, instead of, but preferably together with, internationalization. Therefore, further research is needed to ascertain the validity and generalizability of the arguments and results herein.

Conclusion

This chapter scrutinizes the view of a matrix being a multi-hierarchical structure that possesses substantial advantages. In contrast, we offer the view that MNC matrices are not multi-hierarchical, but mainly single hierarchical. In the MNC matrix, multiple structural dimensions offering multiple information processing channels may exist only at a single level in the hierarchy, in the level immediately reporting to the CEO. Therefore, the matrix advantage is limited.

For a set of German MNCs, the empirical results support the newer view. The limited matrix advantage is shown in the limited advantage in MNC internationalization of matrix structures compared with elementary structures: foreign sales, foreign manufacturing, and intracompany transfers. This limited matrix advantage is quite well predicted by a partially additive model, which is consistent with the matrix being a single hierarchy. Matrices have some advantage over simpler structures, but it is only modest and compatible with their existing at only a single level in the organizational hierarchy.

References

Abdel-Khalik, A. R. 1988. Hierarchies and size: A problem of identification. *Organization Studies* 9 (2):237–51.

Barker, J., D. Tjosvold, and I. R. Andrews. 1988. Conflict approaches and effective and ineffective project managers: A field study in a matrix organization. *Journal of Management Studies* 25 (2):167–78.

Blau, P. M. and R. A. Schoenherr. 1971. *The structure of organizations*. New York: Basic Books.

Burton, R. M., B. Obel, and D. D. Håkonsson. 2015. How to get the matrix organization to work. *Journal of Organization Design* 4 (3):37–45.

Chandler, A. D. 1962. *Strategy and structure: Chapters in the history of the American industrial enterprise*. Cambridge, MA: MIT Press.

Cheng, J. L. C. 1983. Interdependence and coordination in organizations: A role-system analysis. *Academy of Management Journal* 26 (1):156–62.

Cheng, J. L. C., W. J. Henisz, K. Roth, and A. Swaminathan. 2009. From the editors: Advancing interdisciplinary research in the field of international business: Prospects, issues and challenges. *Journal of International Business Studies* 40:1070–74.

Chi, T. and P. Nystrom. 1998. An economic analysis of matrix structure, using multinational corporations as an illustration. *Managerial and Decision Economics* 19 (3):141–56.

Daniels, J. D., R. A. Pitts, and M. J. Tretter. 1984. Strategy and structure of U.S. multinationals: An exploratory study. *Academy of Management Journal* 27 (2):292–307.

Daniels, J. D., R. A. Pitts, and M. J. Tretter. 1985. Organizing for dual strategies of product diversity and international expansion. *Strategic Management Journal* 6 (3):223–37.Davis, S. M. and P. R. Lawrence. 1977. *Matrix*. Reading, MA: Addison-Wesley.

Davison, B. 2003. Management span of control: How wide is too wide? *Journal of Business Strategy* 24 (4):22–29.

Donaldson, L. 2001. *The contingency theory of organizations*. Thousand Oaks, CA: Sage.

Donaldson, L. 2009. In search of the matrix advantage: A reexamination of the fit of matrix structures to transnational strategy. In *Managing subsidiary dynamics: Headquarters role, capability development, and China strategy. Advances in International Management Series*. Cheng, J. L. C., E. Maitland, and S. Nicholas, eds. Bingley, UK: Emerald Publishing.

Dunning, J. and P. Robson. 1987. Multinational corporate integration and regional economic integration. *Journal of Common Market Studies* 26 (2):103–25.

Egelhoff, W. G. 1982. Strategy and structure in multinational corporations: An information processing approach. *Administrative Science Quarterly* 27 (3):435–58.

Egelhoff, W. G. 1988a. Strategy and structure in multinational corporations: A revision of the Stopford and Wells model. *Strategic Management Journal* 9 (1):1–14.

Egelhoff, W. G. 1988b. *Organizing the multinational enterprise: An information processing perspective*. Cambridge, MA: Ballinger.

Egelhoff, W. G. 1991. Information processing theory and the multinational enterprise. *Journal of International Business Studies* 22 (3):341–68.

Elango, B. and C. Pattnaik. 2007. Building capabilities for international operations through networks: A study of Indian firms. *Journal of international business studies* 38 (4):541–55.

Ford, R. and W. Randolph. 1992. Cross-functional structures: A review and integration of matrix organization and project management. *Journal of Management* 18 (2):267–94.

Franko, L. 1976. *The European multinationals*. Stamford, CT: Greylock Publishers.

Galbraith, J. R. 2002. *Designing dynamic organizations: A hands-on guide for leaders at all levels*. New York: AMACOM.

Galbraith, J. R. 2009. *Designing matrix organizations that actually work: How IBM, Proctor & Gamble, and others design for success*. San Francisco, CA: Jossey-Bass.

Galbraith, J. and R. Kazanjian. 1986. Organizing to implement strategies of diversity and globalization: The role of matrix designs. *Human Resource Management* 25 (1):37–54.

Garvin, D. and L. Levesque. 2006. Executive decision making at general motors. *Harvard Business School Case*, 305–26.

Goggin, W. C. 1974. How the multidimensional structure works at Dow Corning. *Harvard Business Review* 55 (1):54–65.

Jones, G. 2001. *Organizational theory, design, and change: Text and cases*. New Jersey: Pearson Education Inc.

Knight, K. 1976. Matrix organization: A review. *Journal of Management Studies* 13 (2): 111–30.

Kolodny, H. 1981. Managing in a matrix. *Business Horizons* 24 (2):17–35.

Larson, E. W. and D. H. Gobeli. 1987. Matrix management: Contradictions and insights. *California Management Review* 29 (4):126–38.

Morschett, D., H. Schramm-Klein, and J. Zentes. 2010. *Strategic international management: Text and cases*. Weisbaden: Gabler.

Nohria, N. and S. Ghoshal. 1997. *The differentiated network: organizing multinational corporations for value creation*. San Francisco, CA: Jossey-Bass.

Piskorski, M. and A. Spadini. 2007. Procter & Gamble: Organization 2005. *Harvard Business School Case*, 707.

Qian, G. and J. Li. 1998. Multinationality, global market diversification, and risk performance for the largest US firms. *Journal of International Management* 4 (2):149–70.

Qiu, J. and L. Donaldson. 2010. The cubic contingency model: Toward a more comprehensive international strategy-structure model. *Journal of General Management* 36 (3):81–100.

Qiu, J. and L. Donaldson. 2012. Stopford and Wells were right! MNC matrix structures do fit a "high-high" strategy. *Management International Review* 52 (5):671–89.

Roth, K., D. Schweiger, and A. Morrison. 1991. Global strategy implementation at the business unit level: Operational capabilities and administrative mechanisms. *Journal of International Business Studies* 22:369–402.

Sanders, W. G. and M. A. Carpenter. 1998. Internationalization and firm governance: The roles of CEO compensation, top team composition, and board structure. *Academy of Management Journal* 41 (2):158–78.

Segal-Horn, S. and D. Faulkner. 2010. *Understanding global strategy*. UK: Cengage Learning EMEA.

Shapira, Z. 2011. I've got a theory paper—Do you? Conceptual, empirical, and theoretical contributions to knowledge in the organizational sciences. *Organization Science* 22 (5):1312–21.

Stopford, J. M. and L. T. Wells. 1972. *Managing the multinational enterprise*. New York: Basic Books.

Wiersema, M. F. and H. P. Bowen. 2008. Corporate diversification: The impact of foreign competition, industry globalization, and product diversification. *Strategic Management Journal* 29 (2):115–32.

Wolf, J. and W. G. Egelhoff. 2002. Research notes and commentaries: A reexamination and extension of international strategy-structure theory. *Strategic Management Journal* 23 (2):181–89.

Wolf, J., W. G. Egelhoff, and M. Adzic. 2007. *Strategy and structure in matrix MNCs*. Paper to Academy of Management annual meeting. Philadelphia, PA.

6 Building Higher-Level Contingency Theory to Reconcile Contradictions between Lower-Level Theories

William Egelhoff and Joachim Wolf

Introduction

Much of the literature that deals with organization and management theory exists as collections of largely disconnected perspectives and theories about various aspects of the broader subject. Research and inquiry into the subject often begins with widely different assumptions about the nature of human behavior and the way it is or should be organized. Contributing to the divide, empirical research has generated a lot of discontinuous and often inconsistent results that have never been reconciled. To a large extent, this is the result of opportunistic foraging in existing databases (the most available form of empirical research) and an exaggerated search for novelty in the findings (a common requirement for publication). Related to this observation, Donaldson (1995) has already described the proliferation of paradigms in organization theory over the recent past. The purpose of this chapter is not to explore the extent of this situation, but to discuss how organization theory might be improved and extended in areas where discontinuous or inconsistent theories that seek to address the same subject already exist.

While the existing state of organization theory reflects the constraints that its academic creators labor under, the aforementioned state of affairs is especially bad for practitioners. They want theory that is consistent and integrated so that appropriate theory can be readily identified and used with confidence. Most practitioners are much more familiar with using the more specified theories from the physical sciences than they are with using theory from the social sciences. Their businesses and technologies often depend directly on the former. For most managers, knowing and using organization theory to guide organizing behavior is discretionary at best. Hearsay and past experience are more important. To make organization theory more usable for practitioners, its domain or area of application needs to be more clearly specified, its inconsistencies need to be reconciled, and it needs to be extended to apply to a wider range of situations.

While the current state and direction of organization theory is not good for practitioners, neither is it good for the long-run interests of academic organization theorists. The long-run goal of most theorists is to make a meaningful and recognized contribution to some theory that continues to be studied by subsequent generations of theorists and practitioners. For this to happen, theory development needs to become more vertical and less horizontal. That is, new theory needs to develop on top of and incorporate existing theory, as opposed to developing on new turf in a way that fails to incorporate or reconcile its development with potentially relevant existing theory. The search for novelty in academic publishing clearly drives horizontal as opposed to vertical theory development. When this kind of horizontal theory development occurs, new theory tends to replace or take the attention away from existing theory. This can lead to a kind of theory "churn," where new theory is not better than existing theory. It is just new or novel. In fact, to the extent that organization theorists have already sought to address the most important aspects of organizing, there is the danger that organization theory may be increasingly addressing ever-more trivial aspects of organizing. To avoid this, it is important that new theory development not lose or fail to integrate the value inherent in existing theory.

It is important to realize that the bounded rationality of humans precludes their learning and using an ever-growing number of organizing theories and conceptual ideas. This is as true for organization theorists as it is for managers in organizations. To improve their potential for organizing, both need better theories and conceptual ideas (more quality, not more quantity). This argues more for the accumulation of knowledge as theory is developed than for the development of totally new knowledge that is discontinuous or largely unrelated to existing knowledge.

We see two fundamentally different ways to attempt to better integrate existing organization theories. The first is to develop some higher-level grand theory that has the power to explain the lower-level theories that are to be reconciled and integrated. This kind of grand theorizing has been responsible for large advances in the physical sciences. For example, the insightful conceptualization associated with the discovery that all matter consists of electrons, protons, and neutrons has reconciled and integrated in a vertical manner many of the previously independent theories that existed in physics and chemistry. This kind of grand, vertically integrated thinking has not found much of an analog in the social sciences, where new theorizing has grown more horizontally.

The second way one might attempt to integrate and reconcile existing organization theories is by developing some kind of higher-level contingency theory that specifies under which condition (which contingencies) one theory or conceptual approach is superior to another. This way does not provide the fundamental new understanding that grand theory provides, but it moves in the direction of grand theory by providing another vertical level of decision making that integrates across the two or more theories or conceptual frameworks that one is attempting to combine. Since the prospects for developing grand theory are poor, this chapter will focus on the prospects for developing a higher-level contingency theory to integrate and reconcile existing organization theory.

The next section will describe in more detail what we mean by a higher-level contingency theory that can reconcile and integrate two conflicting theories or perspectives of organization design. The following section will provide a detailed example of such a higher-level contingency theory, one which attempts to reconcile and integrate the hierarchical coordination and network coordination perspectives. The subsequent section generalizes from this example and attempts to provide some general guidance on how to develop such higher-level contingency theories. A concluding section discusses the benefits that such higher-level contingency theories can potentially provide.

Designing Higher-Level Contingency Theories of Organization Design

The fundamental idea of contingency theory, as it is applied to organizations, is that organizational performance is contingent on the fit between an organization's design and its environment (Donaldson 2001). The term "contingency theory" seems to have originated from the well-known study by Lawrence and Lorsch (1967). This study established that the degrees of differentiation and integration inherent in a firm's organization design need to fit the levels of uncertainty and complexity in its environment for performance to be good. Thus in the original Lawrence and Lorsch model, or contingency theory, performance is the dependent variable, and the contingency variable is the degree of fit between an organization's design and its environment. It is important to note that many contingency theory studies have used this same terminology in a somewhat different way. In most of the subsequent literature, the characteristics of organization design are generally considered the dependent variable, while the characteristics of the environment or strategy are considered the contingency variables. The present chapter will follow this latter convention.

All contingency theory models of organization design relate some characteristic of organization design to one or more characteristics of a firm's environment or strategy. The earliest contingency theory studies tended to be unique in terms of the dependent variables and contingency variables that they studied (Burns and Stalker 1961; Lawrence and Lorsch 1967). But soon standardization set in, and many researchers studied the same dependent variable or organizational characteristic, using the same or similar sets of contingency variables. For example, the formal structure of MNCs has been widely studied for a long period of time (Donaldson 2009; Egelhoff 1982; Egelhoff, Wolf, and Adzic 2013; Franko 1976; Habib and Victor 1991; Qiu and Donaldson 2010, 2012; Stopford and Wells 1972; Wolf and Egelhoff 2002). As a result of so much comparable study, a good deal of useful theory has developed about the appropriate way to fit type of formal structure to the key characteristics of a firm's environment and strategy. Although perhaps less developed, similar theories also exist for fitting other characteristics of organization design, such as degree of centralization (Garnier 1982; Gates and Egelhoff 1986; Hedlund 1981), control processes (Brandt and Hulbert 1976; Youssef 1975), and staffing policies (Edstrom and Galbraith 1979; Jaeger 1983; Toyne and Kuehne 1983) to a firm's environment and strategy.

We consider all of the aforementioned contingency theories to be foundation contingency theories. They typically relate some directly measurable characteristic of organization design to some directly measurable characteristic of the firm's environment or strategy. It is important to observe that within such foundation contingency theories, the values of the dependent variable or organization design characteristic are generally easy to compare: a functional-division structure versus a product-division structure, or a high level of centralization versus a lower level of centralization. In other words, the different values of the dependent variable all refer to a similar coordinating mechanism: a hierarchical structure, where in the hierarchy decisions are made. This is important, because we now want to introduce the situation where the values of the dependent variable or organization design characteristic are not so comparable, because they do not refer to a similar coordinating mechanism. Examples of this are whether to use a hierarchy or a market to coordinate an activity and whether to use a hierarchy or a network to coordinate an activity. In both cases, the values of the dependent variable or organization design characteristic (hierarchy versus market, hierarchy versus network) are not so easy to compare. In both cases, they are not simply variants of a similar coordinating mechanism, as is the case with most foundation contingency theories. Instead, what needs to be evaluated and compared are two different types of coordinating mechanism. When this situation exists, we will argue that one needs a different kind of contingency theory—a higher-level contingency theory—to facilitate comparing and reconciling the more difficult to compare values of the dependent variable or organization design characteristic. This situation occurs whenever one seeks to consider, simultaneously, two foundation theories or perspectives that are discontinuous and inconsistent.

An illustrative example of such higher-level theory reconciling and integrating previously discontinuous and often conflicting perspectives is the emergence in the 1970s of what is commonly called markets and hierarchies theory (Milgrom and Roberts 1992; Williamson 1975, 1991). Markets and hierarchies (with central planning as a key characteristic of hierarchy) are two fundamentally different ways of coordinating economic activity. Both can operate at the level of the economy (global and national) and the firm. Prior to the emergence of markets and hierarchies theory, there was no defined way to decide which mode of coordination was superior to the other. At the level of the economy, some economists argued for the advantages of free markets (Friedman 1962; Hayek 1945), while others argued for more centrally planned economies (Keynes 2006). At the level of the firm, most organization and management theorists argued for some form of hierarchical coordination, while a minority argued for a greater use of internal markets within firms (Ackoff 1993; Cowen and Parker 1997; Ellig 2001; Halal 1994; Magidson and Polcha 1992). Generally, these arguments simply passed by each other without much reference or contact. They did not reconcile and integrate the two perspectives; they did not recombine knowledge in a way that could inform practitioners when one form of coordination might be superior to the other.

Markets and hierarchies theory (Milgrom and Roberts 1992; Williamson 1975, 1991), however, does attempt to specify when one mode of coordination will be superior to the other. It accomplishes this by leaving the theory associated with markets and the theory associated with hierarchy intact. It then builds a new higher-level contingency theory on top of these two foundation theories. The dependent variable of the new contingency theory is mode of coordination, and it has two values (use hierarchical coordination and use market coordination). The contingency variable of the new theory is the transaction costs associated with coordinating a transaction or exchange. If the transaction costs associated with coordinating a specific type of transaction with market coordination is lower than the transaction costs associated with coordinating it with hierarchical coordination, the economy or firm should use market coordination. Since both economies and firms embrace many different types of transactions, the optimal coordination design is likely to be some specific mixture of market and hierarchical coordination. This is a result that neither of the two foundation theories could have provided. The new higher-level contingency theory says that neither of the two previously competing foundation theories will be optimal for all situations (all types of transactions). It provides new insight into why transaction costs and problems are likely to increase if the wrong mode of coordination is used. This is how the new higher-level contingency theory reconciles and integrates the two foundation theories or perspectives.

Operationalizing and measuring the contingency variable (the transaction costs associated with a specific type of transaction) is more abstract and complex than directly measuring the contingency variable for most foundation contingency theories. Typically, one cannot sum the various transaction costs associated with using a hierarchy to coordinate a given transaction and compare it against the summed transaction costs associated with using a market to coordinate the same transaction. Instead, one tends to identify the most critical transaction costs associated with the transaction (from a list of potential transaction costs already identified by markets and hierarchies theory) and then evaluate qualitatively which mode of coordination (a hierarchy or a market) is associated with the lowest or most acceptable set of transaction costs. The analysis can be difficult and open to criticism, but a good deal of well-established and generally accepted logic for making such decisions does exist (Milgrom and Roberts 1992). Our purpose in introducing this theory is not to evaluate it, but to use it as an illustration—to view it as an attempt to construct a higher-level contingency theory that seeks to reconcile and integrate two underlying foundation theories that are discontinuous and conflicting. This is the phenomenon the present chapter seeks to explore and better understand. In the next section, we will describe in much greater detail the development of a second higher-level contingency theory. It is a theory that seeks to reconcile the theories that deal with hierarchies and networks.

A Detailed Example of Discontinuous and Inconsistent Theories and the Higher-Level Contingency Theory That Seeks to Address Them

An important example of discontinuous and inconsistent theories that seek to address the same subject can be found in the debate over the use of hierarchical coordination as opposed to network coordination in large, complex organizations such as multinational corporations (MNCs). A hierarchical connection is between a superordinate and a subordinate, whereas a network connection is between peers. Early research and theory tended to emphasize the importance of formal hierarchical structure for the coordination of such firms (Chandler 1962; Egelhoff 1982; Stopford and Wells 1972). Later research and theory has questioned the importance of hierarchical coordination and has instead put more emphasis on the use of nonhierarchical network coordination in such firms (Bartlett and Ghoshal 1989; Birkinshaw and Hagstrom 2000; Ghoshal and Nohria 1997; Hedlund 1986). This debate has never been resolved in a way that leads to a deeper understanding of how to organize and coordinate MNCs.

Most recent research and theorizing has focused on the use of network coordination in firms while ignoring or minimizing the role of hierarchical coordination (Ambos, Andersson, and Birkinshaw 2010; Andersson, Forsgren, and Holm 2007; Balogun, Jarzabkowski, and Vaara 2011; Birkinshaw, Hood, and Young 2005; Bouquet and Birkinshaw 2008; Ciabuschi, Forsgren, and Martin Martin 2012; Ciabuschi, Martin Martin, and Stahl 2010; Foss, Foss, and Nell 2012; Mudambi and Navarra 2004). At the same time, a modest amount of research and theorizing has continued to argue for the importance of hierarchical coordination in MNCs (Egelhoff, Wolf, and Adzic 2013; Qiu and Donaldson 2010, 2012; Wolf and Egelhoff 2002). But overall, network coordination is clearly replacing hierarchical coordination when it comes to theorizing about the coordination of large, complex organizations such as MNCs. Since theorists and practitioners tend to be more aware of recent theorizing than of old theorizing, there is a danger that useful insight and understanding about hierarchical coordination will be generally ignored and lost. If this occurs, it would be an example of theory churn.

A recent article by Egelhoff (2010) develops a higher-level contingency theory that seeks to address the aforementioned problem. The contingency theory seeks to reconcile and integrate the arguments of the two opposing theories by trying to specify under what conditions (what contingencies) hierarchical coordination would be superior to network coordination, and vice versa. To the extent the model succeeds in specifying these conditions, it reconciles and keeps alive and relevant the valuable knowledge contained in both theories. The remainder of this section will describe enough of the logic underlying the new higher-level contingency model so that the reader can understand and critically evaluate the effort to develop such a model. This is the subject of the present chapter. While the illustrated example will produce a model of when to use hierarchical coordination and when to use network coordination, readers who are interested in this specific subject should read Egelhoff (2010), which discusses more fully the context of the model and its implications for hierarchical and network coordination in MNCs.

Egelhoff (2010) uses an information processing perspective of organization design. Information processing in organizations is generally defined as including the gathering of data, the transformation of data into information, and the communication and storage of information in the organization (Egelhoff 1991; Galbraith 1973; Tushman and Nadler 1978). Different kinds of organization design (a hierarchical structure, a network structure) possess different information processing capacities. Different strategies and tasks in a firm create different information processing requirements. A particular organization design or structure is effective when its information processing capacities fit the information processing requirements of the strategy or task it is attempting to coordinate.

The Information Processing Capacities of Hierarchical and Network Structures

A hierarchical structure uses the chain of command to process information and provide coordination. It is capable of providing non-routine information processing, but vulnerable to information processing overload (Egelhoff 1988). From an information processing perspective, the most important attributes of organizational hierarchy are vertical specialization and centralization. Vertical specialization provides a difference in perspective (a strategic versus a tactical perspective) that is generally not available from a nonhierarchical form of organization. Centralization of decision making facilitates the aggregating of diverse information (from different horizontal subunits and different vertical levels) for comprehensive decision making. Again, this is a relatively unique capability of the hierarchy.

The general concept of a network structure embraces a variety of conceptualizations of nonhierarchical form in the organizational literature: heterarchy (Hedlund 1986), multifocal firm (Prahalad and Doz 1987), interorganizational network (Ghoshal and Bartlett 1990), horizontal organization (White and Poynter 1990), transnational firm (Bartlett and Ghoshal 1989), network-based structures (Malnight 1996), differentiated network (Ghoshal and Nohria 1997). Although there may be subtle differences among these, most forms are not sufficiently specified to make these differences clear or meaningful. In an MNC with a network structure, subsidiaries tend to directly process information with each other, as opposed to going through HQ under a more hierarchical hub-and-spoke design. Each subsidiary develops and becomes embedded in its own external network of suppliers and customers (Forsgren, Holm, and Johanson 2005). This exposes most subunits to divergent pulls from inside and outside of the firm. The result is a more fluid and market-like shifting of power and resources across the subunits of a firm. The internal network becomes an arena for creation and experimentation rather than just for the exploitation of given knowledge and other resources (Hedlund 1993). Internal networks facilitate learning through problem solving among subsidiaries that are complementary and knowledge transfer between subsidiaries that are similar (Forsgren, Holm, and Johanson 2005). Thus the network structure is a radically different organizational design from the hierarchical structure. These differences are summarized in Table 6.1.

Table 6.1 Important Differences between Hierarchical Structures and Network Structures That Influence Their Information Processing Capacities

Hierarchical structure	*Network structure*
Goal structure	
• Strategic firm-level goals held by HQ. Diverse subunit goals held by subunits.	• Diverse subunit goals held by subunits. Unclear how firm-level goals will arise without some hierarchy.
• Provides a reasonable level of goal congruence across levels and subunits along the organizing dimension.	• Primary mechanism for achieving congruence is shared vision and firm-level culture.
Information flows	
• Formal information flows along the hierarchy are directed by fiat; augmenting informal flows develop from high position familiarity and trust.	• Information flows among subunits are voluntary, informal, and flexible; they are influenced more by personal familiarity and trust than by position familiarity.
• Hierarchies centralize information as it moves up and becomes more strategic and disperse it as it moves down and becomes more tactical.	• Networks can take many shapes, so there is no single pattern to the shaping of information flows.
Motivation and behavior	
• Provides a system of incentives that supports extrinsic motivation and the processing of explicit (as opposed to tacit) information.	• Facilitates intrinsic motivation and the development and transfer of tacit knowledge.
Decision making	
• Tends to push decisions up the hierarchy when there is interdependency across subunits.	• Tends to keep decisions at the subunit level and exchange the necessary information to take interdependency into account.
• Tends to standardize many decisions (often through centralization) to reduce complexity and achieve efficiency.	• Tends to tolerate diversity in decisions and decision making.
• Facilitates centralized, comprehensive decision making by a HQ (where firm-level goals and knowledge are more important than subunit goals and knowledge).	• Facilitates decentralized, incremental decision making by the local subunits (where subunit goals and knowledge are more important than firm-level goals and knowledge).

Reproduced from Egelhoff (2010)

Goal Structure

Goals and plans help to inform and coordinate the actions of subunits within a firm. The goal structures associated with hierarchical structures and network structures are likely to be quite different. In an organizational hierarchy, there tends to be a hierarchy of goals. HQ primarily identifies and works with strategic and other firm-level goals, while subunits largely identify and work with more local subunit goals. This implies a difference in HQ and subunit perspectives. A HQ will generally use its institutional power to ensure some reasonable level of goal congruence between the diverse subunit goals and the overall firm-level goals. This congruence will tend to exist along the organizing dimension of a structure, while there may well be incongruence along other dimensions not emphasized by the hierarchical structure.

In a network structure without any hierarchical structure, it is unclear how firm-level goals will arise. Local subunits' goals will tend to evolve to fit the local situations. In the literature on networks, the primary mechanism for achieving goal congruence across subunits or with some firm-level goal seems to be shared vision (Bartlett and Ghoshal 1989) or firm-level culture (Edstrom and Galbraith 1979). But the emergence and existence of shared vision and firm-level culture is not specified in the networks' literature; it is largely assumed. Thus the network-structure perspective seems to be associated with a rather incomplete picture of how firm-level goals develop and evolve within MNCs.

Information Flows

The mechanisms influencing information flows in hierarchies and networks are also fundamentally different. The formal flows of information within a hierarchy are largely directed by fiat (Williamson 1975). This makes them reliable and predictable. The levels and subunits in a hierarchy tend to be mutually familiar with each other. They are familiar with who is responsible for something, who knows something, and who needs to know. Much of this kind of familiarity relates more to the positions in a hierarchy than to the actual persons filling the positions. Familiarity, frequent interaction, and goal congruence within a hierarchy leads to trust—trust that information will be conscientiously provided and properly attended to. Despite the maladies of hierarchies, both familiarity and trust are generally greater within a hierarchy than between individuals or subunits not linked by a hierarchy. When familiarity and trust are high within a hierarchy, there is generally a high level of informal information flow within the hierarchy, which parallels and enriches the formal information flows. The shape of a hierarchy naturally centralizes information as it moves up and becomes more strategic, and it disperses information as it moves down and becomes more tactical.

In contrast to a hierarchy, there is little formally specified information flow in most network structures. Instead, information flow is largely informal and voluntary, driven by the need to coordinate interdependent tasks or address mutual problems (Forsgren, Holm, and Johanson 2005; Hedlund 1986). Information flow in a network will depend heavily upon personal familiarity and trust between the nodes, since organizational positions and position familiarity has reduced meaning outside of a hierarchy. Unlike a hierarchy, a network structure has no fixed shape, so it can potentially accommodate a wide variety of information flow patterns. Since all information networks depend on some kind of familiarity between the nodes, the variety and density of specific information flow networks within a network structure will depend heavily upon the degree of familiarity among the subunit nodes.

Motivation and Behavior

Hierarchies are more strongly associated with providing extrinsic motivation than intrinsic motivation. With such incentives as pay and promotion deliberately linked to realizing the formal hierarchical goals of the firm, extrinsic motivation is very powerful in many firms. There is even some empirical evidence that strong extrinsic motivation can "crowd out" intrinsic motivation in organizations (Deci 1975; Lepper and Greene 1978), as it preempts the limited attention and focus of employees. Extrinsic motivation favors the development and transfer of explicit information over the development and transfer of tacit knowledge, since the former can be monitored and rewarded (Osterloh and Frey 2000). Thus hierarchies are better designed to process explicit information than tacit knowledge.

Network structures, on the other hand, are associated with supporting intrinsic motivation and the development and transfer of tacit knowledge (Osterloh and Frey 2000). When the network structure is applied to an MNC, most of the extrinsic motivation resides at the subunit level. Above this level, relationships tend to be more informal and voluntary, and there is more opportunity for intrinsic motivation to exert its influence. Thus network structures should be superior to hierarchical structures in facilitating the development and transfer of tacit knowledge in MNCs.

Decision Making

Decision making is also quite different under a hierarchy and a network structure. When there is interdependency across subunits so that information from various subunits has to be combined to make a decision, a hierarchy will tend to centralize the decision making above the subunit level. Facing the same situation, a network structure will attempt to exchange the necessary information among the subunits and either jointly arrive at a decision or allow each subunit to individually make its own decision based on the same shared information. This centralized versus decentralized approach to handling interdependency has different consequences for different situations.

In a hierarchy, there is also a tendency to standardize many decisions across the subunits. This reduces the complexity and information processing requirements faced by an HQ, but it may result in insufficient sensitivity to local differences at the subunit level. A network structure generally decentralizes most decisions to the subunit level and tolerates diversity in decisions and decision-making styles. This provides a lot of sensitivity to local differences, but leads to a more complex, heterogeneous, and less consistent decision-making environment within the firm. Accordingly, a hierarchy facilitates centralized, comprehensive decision making, where firm-level goals and contextual knowledge are more important to the decision than subunit goals and knowledge. Conversely, a network structure facilitates more decentralized, incremental decision making, where subunit-level goals and knowledge are of primary importance.

The Information Processing Requirements of Tasks

Having specified and distinguished the information processing capacities of hierarchical and network structures, Egelhoff (2010) subsequently evaluates which types of tasks each type of structure can best fit based on the information processing requirements associated with the task. The approach evaluates hypothetical examples of various types of tasks. The conclusion is that hierarchical structures are superior to network structures in providing coordination for three broad types of tasks: (1) designing and implementing tight coupling among subunits, (2) identifying and defining economies of scale and scope, and (3) identifying and incorporating significant innovation into firm strategy.

Coordinating tightly coupled systems, where there is high interdependency among the subunits and no independency (Orton and Weick 1990), requires that most information be moved to a central point so that comprehensive decision making that optimizes firm-level performance can occur. This fits the information processing capacities of a hierarchical structure with a HQ. Egelhoff (2010) contrasts this with an example that can be better coordinated with a network structure. Coordination problems that require that some aggregation of subunit-level knowledge be combined with the local knowledge of a specific subunit, where the latter is more difficult to transfer, are well suited to a network structure design. Such problems require independency among the subunits to respect the variation in local knowledge, and they require interdependency to construct and leverage the required body of aggregated common knowledge. A network structure fits this situation precisely because it is a loosely coupled system, which by definition embraces some degree of interdependency and some degree of independency (Orton and Weick 1990).

> *Proposition 1:* Developing and implementing tight coupling of subunit behaviors across a firm is best coordinated with a hierarchical

structure, while the loose coupling of subunit behaviors is best coordinated with a network structure.

Identifying and defining the potential for realizing economies of scale or scope for some component or service within a firm requires bringing together information about the supply costs and demand revenues of the component or service. As the number of subunits increases, it becomes increasingly difficult for the horizontal information processing capacity of a network structure to accomplish this task. On the other hand, the vertical information processing capacity of a hierarchical structure is well suited to accomplishing this task, even when the number of subunits and volume of data become very large.

Proposition 2: Hierarchical structures are superior to network structures in identifying and defining economies of scale and scope.

Identifying and incorporating significant innovation into firm strategies also requires bringing the relevant information together at a central point and evaluating it in a comprehensive manner. This is the same requirement that was associated with the economies of scale problem. It will be more difficult for a network to accomplish this, and there may also be a tendency for subunits in a network to make decisions incrementally before a comprehensive evaluation has occurred. The second reason for preferring a hierarchical structure is that it adds increased vertical specialization to the decision process. It will be easier for HQ managers in a hierarchy to assume a longer time horizon and view new innovation as discontinuous from the present since they do not have to manage current operations directly. Subunit managers in a network organization, on the other hand, will have primary responsibility for current operations and performance. It would be natural for them to see the future as continuous with the present. In a mature industry with little prospect of significant change this may be fine, but it will be inappropriate if a firm faces significant new innovations. The advantage a hierarchical structure has over a network structure is that it can simultaneously support more radically different views of the present and future organization.

Proposition 3: Hierarchical structures are superior to network structures in identifying and incorporating significant new innovation into firm strategies.

The view expressed earlier may appear to contradict some of the virtues currently attributed to network structures. Some scholars believe that a lot of innovation either enters or could potentially enter an MNC through its network of foreign subsidiaries (Birkinshaw 2000; Forsgren, Holm, and Johanson 2005). A critical part of this view is the embeddedness of subsidiaries in their local environments, whereby they pick up new innovative knowledge, which can be distributed and further developed through a network structure. Birkinshaw (2000), for example, argues that a good deal of new firm-level strategy should emerge from such subsidiary initiatives. Our view is that while subsidiary-level initiatives that seek to alter corporate-level strategy might initially be generated by a network structure, they should be further developed and adopted through a hierarchical structure rather than through a horizontal network structure. This exposes the new initiatives or innovations to a more comprehensive evaluation and a different perspective, as discussed earlier.

In order to reconcile these seemingly opposing views—that networks and hierarchies both contribute to the level of new innovation in an MNC—it is necessary to further conceptualize the specific contributions of each. New innovations originating at the subsidiary level are often associated with a good deal of tacit knowledge (about customers, supply chains, production processes, and product technologies). To develop such knowledge further to the point where it can be identified and evaluated as a new innovation, different kinds of network information processing are usually required. Cross-functional networks within subsidiaries allow an idea that might have originated within a single function to be tested from different functional perspectives (R&D, manufacturing, marketing). Functional networks between subsidiaries (an R&D network, manufacturing network, and marketing network, each across subsidiaries) allows a higher level of functional specialization and experience effects to modify and enrich the original idea. External networks with customers, suppliers, and competitors surround each subsidiary and also inform new innovations at the subsidiary level. This kind of flexible network information processing exposes new ideas to a potentially wide variety of inputs, increasing the chance that some valuable recombination of knowledge will occur. Since all transfers of knowledge encourage making it more explicit, the time innovations spend in subsidiary-level networks also helps to codify innovative knowledge so that a hierarchy can vertically transmit it. This line of reasoning leads to the following proposition:

> *Proposition 4:* The level of new innovations generated at the subsidiary level of an MNC will be positively influenced by (1) the density of cross-functional (and cross-product) networks within subsidiaries, (2) the density of functional (or product) networks that exist across subsidiaries, and (3) the embeddedness of subsidiaries within local environments (external networks between subsidiaries and local environments).

The earlier discussion describes the creation or generation phase of bottom-up innovations in MNCs. For such innovations to be incorporated into firm-level strategy, the information processing perspective would argue that they should subsequently undergo an evaluation and selection phase that involves hierarchical information processing. As already discussed, this subjects the new ideas to a review that involves a firm-level strategic perspective, which tends to differ from the perspectives that were present during the generation phase. For example, imagine a new product innovation that has been generated by one or more subsidiaries of an MNC. As this innovation requires more resources (to develop, produce, market), it will typically be transmitted up some kind of hierarchy within the MNC. This hierarchical information processing will evaluate and probably modify the innovation before it is included in the MNC's firm-level strategy. If the innovation moves up the hierarchy of a worldwide product-division structure, there will be a tendency to globally standardize the product, design the product for a few major markets, and realize global economies of scale in sourcing and production. These are the goals and perspectives that a product-division hierarchy typically brings to the task. Subsidiary-level innovations that are not valued by this perspective are likely to be rejected and discouraged by such a hierarchy. On the other hand, if the same innovation moves up a geographical region hierarchy, there will be a tendency to regionally standardize the product (with tolerance for local variations varying by region), design the product for a wider range of markets, and forego global economies of scale.

As illustrated earlier, changing the hierarchical structure changes the way information is aggregated and the kind of vertical specialization (in terms of goals, perspectives, and knowledge) that managers bring to the task of evaluating and incorporating subsidiary-level innovations into higher levels of strategy. Subsidiary-level innovations that are rejected by one type of hierarchical structure may be embraced by another type, and the ways different types of hierarchical structure further develop and incorporate such innovations into firm-level strategy differ significantly. Since one of these outcomes is likely to be superior to the others in terms of the firm-level advantages it provides, it is important for an MNC to have the most appropriate or suitable hierarchical structure in place. This line of reasoning leads to the following proposition:

> *Proposition 5:* The level of subsidiary-generated new innovations selected for inclusion in an MNC's firm-level strategy will be positively influenced by (1) the level of new innovations generated and codified as explicit knowledge and (2) the existence of a suitable hierarchy (functional, product, geographic) for transmitting and evaluating new innovations above the subsidiary level.

Thus the proposed reconciling argument is that network structures facilitate the generation of subsidiary-level innovations, while suitable hierarchical structures are critical to the selection and incorporation of such innovations into MNC strategy.

Generalizing from the Example

The aforementioned example describes the development of a higher-level contingency theory that both reconciles and integrates the hierarchical structure and network structure theories of coordination. These were previously independent theories of organizing that are generally regarded as contradictory approaches when they are used to address the same problem—how to organize a firm. The new higher-level contingency theory essentially says that it is wrong to apply these two foundation theories or conceptual perspectives to the same coordination problem. Instead, some problems will be better addressed by hierarchical structure theory, while other problems will be better addressed by network structure theory. The new higher-level contingency theory effectively changes the level of analysis for applying the two foundation theories from the level of the firm to the level of the task. Coordination for certain types of tasks can be better addressed using hierarchical structure theory, while other types of tasks can be better addressed with network structure theory. Re-specifying the proper domains of the foundation theories is the real contribution of a higher-level contingency theory. Without such a theory, there is a natural tendency to apply the foundation theories to all of the tasks in a firm. This tendency has led to conflict between the two theories that is dysfunctional—dysfunctional in the sense that little new understanding or insight has come out of the debate and there is no clear advice for practitioners who want to apply the theory.

A higher-level contingency theory always changes the level of analysis for applying the lower-level foundation theories. It always lowers the level of analysis so that each of the previously competing theories can now be assigned a separate and narrower domain for its application. Since it is easier to develop sound theory for a simpler domain than for a more complex domain, the development of higher-level contingency theory should also facilitate the subsequent development of the foundation theories. It does this by more precisely specifying the domain to which a specific foundation theory applies. This line of reasoning suggests that conflicting theories about organizing frequently result from inadequate or insufficient domain specification. Attempting to develop a new higher-level contingency theory is largely an effort to discover and specify a further level of domain definition.

The central problem associated with constructing a higher-level contingency theory is how to identify and define the best contingency variable (or variables). The best contingency variable is the one that will most insightfully distinguish between the domains of the foundation theories that one is attempting to reconcile and integrate. Transaction costs theory argues that the transaction costs associated with markets and hierarchies tend to be the best contingency variable for further specifying the proper domains of each. In an analogous manner, information processing theory argues that the information processing characteristics associated with hierarchies and networks tend to be the best contingency variable for further specifying the proper domains of these two modes of coordination.

It is important to observe that higher-level contingency theories are distinguishing between the domains of competing theories and perspectives, while lower-level contingency theories are distinguishing between alternative values of a dependent variable that lies within the bounds of a single theory or perspective (e.g., a high level of centralization versus a low level of centralization). Identifying and defining a contingency variable for a lower-level contingency theory is easier than doing the same for a higher-level contingency theory. It is more likely to be something that can be directly observed and measured (e.g., the number of employees in a firm). The higher-level contingency variable, on the other hand, is likely to be more abstract and difficult to define and measure.

The contingency variable that seeks to reconcile the separate theories associated with hierarchies and networks is the type of task that needs to be coordinated. Describing the types of tasks that can be better coordinated with a hierarchy as opposed to a network requires a lengthy, multidimensional response. This occurs because the contingency variable, type of task, is a nominal variable. Each type of task is different, and there is no identifiable common scale or dimension that explains their variation. As a result, a different logic is required to relate each type of task to the values of the dependent variable (hierarchy or network). This situation will occur whenever the contingency variable is a nominal variable, which it frequently is for higher-level contingencies.

Lower-level contingency theories, on the other hand, tend to have contingency variables that are interval-scale or ordinal variables. This leads to a much simpler, more unidimensional explanation of the contingency relationship. This tends to be true even when the dependent variable is nominal, as in the case of structure (functional-division, product-division, and geographic-region structures). When placed in a discriminant analysis, three interval-scale contingency variables (product diversity, size of foreign operations, and size of foreign manufacturing) are capable of accurately discriminating among the three types of structures listed earlier (Egelhoff 1982). In comparison, Table 6.1 describes at least 20 different characteristics that help to distinguish the information processing capabilities of hierarchies and networks. Each of these needs to be considered when attempting to specify and evaluate the information processing requirements of a specific type of task (the values of the contingency variable) against the information processing capabilities of hierarchies and networks (the values of the dependent variable).

A similar situation and conclusion arise when one considers the earlier example involving markets and hierarchies. Here the contingency variable of the higher-level contingency theory (markets and hierarchies theory) is different types of economic transactions. In their summary of markets and hierarchies theory, Milgrom and Roberts (1992) identify a wide variety of different kinds of transaction costs that need to be considered when evaluating whether a specific type of transaction should be coordinated with markets or hierarchies. While such nominal higher-level contingency variables are clearly more difficult to work with, they also imply a potentially richer and more multidimensional understanding of a relationship.

Conclusion

Constructing such higher-level, more-integrating contingency theories provides three important benefits. First, it reduces the number of situations where there are contradicting theories seeking to address the same problem. Such situations frustrate practitioners and generally prevent them from applying any academically derived theory to a problem. This situation also leads to a large amount of dysfunctional debate within academic circles. The second benefit is the preservation of more useful knowledge as it is integrated into higher-level contingency theories that are actively used and further developed. This kind of theory development leads to the accumulation of knowledge as opposed to the sequential replacement of knowledge or "knowledge churn."

The third primary benefit is more usable theory that can address a wider range of problems. One can observe from the earlier example that the resultant higher-level contingency theory integrating hierarchical structure and network structure theory is more than the simple sum of the knowledge and insight contained in the two foundation theories. The explicit identification of the information processing capacities of hierarchical structures as opposed to network structures, as summarized in Table 6.1, provides understanding and insight about coordination that is not present in either of the foundation theories. The fits and misfits between these capacities and the information processing requirements of a variety of tasks leads to additional understanding about the kinds of coordination different tasks require. A couple of rather fundamental insights emerge from the comparative process that develops the higher-level contingency theory. One is that appropriate structure can either bring information together to some central point where it can support well-informed, comprehensive decision making, or it can share and disperse information to support well-informed, decentralized decision making. Another insight is the criticality of the goals, perspectives, and incentives that are operating at the point where decisions are made. These vary considerably across different types of hierarchical structure and different types of network structure. Thus useful higher-level contingency theories can probably provide both wider and deeper insight into a subject.

In conclusion, this chapter has described in some detail one specific attempt to develop a useful higher-level contingency theory that reconciles and integrates two otherwise conflicting theories. It has then sought to generalize from this example and provide some basic guidance on how to develop additional higher-level contingency theory for other areas where there are discontinuous and conflicting organization theories. We believe there is a greater need for this kind of theory development than there is for further horizontal theory development.

References

Ackoff, R. L. 1993. Corporate perestroika: The internal market economy. In *Internal market: Bringing the power of free enterprise inside your organization.* Halal, W. E., A. Geranmayeh, and J. Pourdehnad, eds. New York: Wiley, 15–26.

Ambos, T., U. Andersson, and J. Birkinshaw. 2010. What are the consequences of initiative-taking in multinational subsidiaries? *Journal of International Business Studies* 41:1–20.

Andersson, U., M. Forsgren, and U. Holm. 2007. Balancing subsidiary influence in the federative MNC: A business network view. *Journal of International Business Studies* 38:802–18.

Balogun, J., P. Jarzabkowski, and E. Vaara. 2011. Selling, resistance and reconciliation: A critical discursive approach to subsidiary role evolution in MNEs. *Journal of International Business Studies* 42:765–86.

Bartlett, C. A. and S. Ghoshal. 1989. *Managing across borders: The transnational solution.* Harvard Business School Press, Boston, MA.

Birkinshaw, J. 2000. *Entrepreneurship in the global firm.* Thousand Oaks, CA: Sage.

Birkinshaw, J. and P. Hagstrom. 2000. *The flexible firm: Capability management in network organizations.* Oxford: Oxford University Press.

Birkinshaw, J., N. Hood, and S. Young. 2005. Subsidiary entrepreneurship, internal and external competitive forces, and subsidiary performance. *International Business Review* 14:227–48.

Bouquet, C. and J. Birkinshaw. 2008. Weight versus voice: How foreign subsidiaries gain attention from corporate headquarters. *Academy of Management Journal* 51:577–601.

Brandt, W. K. and J. M. Hulbert. 1976. *A empresa multinacional no Brasil: Um estudo empirico.* Rio de Janeiro: Zahar Editores.

Burns, T. E. & G. M. Stalker. 1961. The management of innovation. *University of Illinois at Urbana-Champaign's Academy for Entrepreneurial Leadership Historical Research Reference in Entrepreneurship.*

Chandler, A. D. 1962. *Strategy and structure: Chapters in the history of industrial enterprise.* Cambridge, MA: MIT Press.

Ciabuschi, F., M. Forsgren, and O. Martin Martin. 2012. Headquarters involvement and efficiency of innovation development and transfer in multinationals: A matter of sheer ignorance? *International Business Review* 21:130–44.

Ciabuschi, F., O. Martin Martin, and B. Stahl. 2010. Headquarters' influence on knowledge transfer performance. *Management International Review* 50:471–91.

Cowen, T. and D. Parker. 1997. *Markets in the firm: A market-process approach to management.* London: Institute of Economic Affairs.

Deci, E. L. 1975. *Intrinsic motivation.* New York: Plenum Press.

Donaldson, L. 1995. *American anti-management theories of organization: A critique of paradigm proliferation.* Cambridge: Cambridge University Press.

Donaldson, L. 2001. *The contingency theory of organizations.* Thousand Oaks, CA: Sage.

Donaldson, L. 2009. In search of the matrix advantage: A re-examination of the fit of matrix structures to transnational strategy in MNEs. In *Managing subsidiary dynamics: Headquarters role, capability development, and China strategy.* Cheng, J., E. Maitland, and S. Nicholas, eds. Bingley, UK: Emerald Publishing, 3–26.

Edstrom, A. and J. Galbraith. 1979. Transfer of managers as a coordination and control device in multinational organizations. *Administrative Science Quarterly* 22:248–63.

Egelhoff, W. G. 1982. Strategy and structure in multinational corporations: An information processing approach. *Administrative Science Quarterly* 27:435–58.

Egelhoff, W. G. 1988. *Organizing the multinational enterprise: An information processing perspective.* Cambridge, MA: Ballinger Publishing.

Egelhoff, W. G. 1991. Information processing theory and the multinational enterprise. *Journal of International Business Studies* 22:341–58.

Egelhoff, W. G. 2010. How the parent headquarters adds value to an MNC. *Management International Review* 50:413–31.

Egelhoff, W. G., J. Wolf, and M. Adzic. 2013. Designing matrix structures to fit MNC strategy. *Global Strategy Journal* 3:205–26.

Ellig, J. 2001. Internal markets and the theory of the firm. *Managerial and Decision Economics* 22:227–37.

Forsgren, M., U. Holm, and J. Johanson. 2005. *Managing the embedded multinational: A business network view.* Cheltenham, UK: Edward Elgar Publishing.

Foss, K., N. J. Foss, and P. C. Nell. 2012. MNC organizational form and subsidiary motivation problems: controlling intervention hazards in the network MNC. *Journal of International Management* 18:247–59.

Franko, L. G. 1976. *The European multinationals: A renewed challenge to American and British big business.* Stamford, CT: Greylock.

Friedman, M. 1962. *Capitalism and freedom.* Chicago: University of Chicago Press.

Galbraith, J. R. 1973. *Designing complex organizations.* Reading, MA: Addison-Wesley.

Garnier, G. H. 1982. Context and decision making autonomy in the foreign affiliates of U.S. multinational corporations. *Academy of Management Journal* 25:893–908.

Gates, S. R. and W. G. Egelhoff. 1986. Centralization in headquarters–subsidiary relationships. *Journal of International Business Studies* 17:71–92.

Ghoshal, S. and C. A. Bartlett. 1990. The multinational corporation as an interorganizational network. *Academy of Management Review* 15:603–35.

Ghoshal, S. and N. Nohria. 1997. *The differentiated MNC: Organizing the multinational corporation for value creation.* San Francisco, CA: Jossey-Bass.

Habib, M. and B. Victor. 1991. Strategy, structure, and performance of U.S. manufacturing and service MNCs. *Strategic Management Journal* 12:589–606.

Halal, W. E. 1994. From hierarchy to enterprise: Internal markets are the new foundation of management. *Academy of Management Executive* 8:69–83.

Hayek, F. A. 1945. The use of knowledge in society. *American Economic Review* 35:519–30.

Hedlund, G. 1981. Autonomy of subsidiaries and formalization of headquarters-subsidiary relationships in Swedish MNCs. In *The management of headquarters-subsidiary relationships in multinational corporations.* Otterbeck, L., ed. New York: St. Martins Press, 25–78.

Hedlund, G. 1986. The hypermodern MNC—A heterarchy? *Human Resource Management* 25:9–35.

Hedlund, G. 1993. Assumptions of hierarchy and heterarchy, with application to the management of the multinational corporation. In *Organization theory and the multinational corporation.* Ghoshal, S. and E. Westney, eds. London: Macmillan, 211–36.

Jaeger, A. M. 1983. The transfer of organizational culture overseas: An approach to control in the multinational corporation. *Journal of International Business Studies*, 14:91–114.

Keynes, J. M. 2006. *General theory of employment, interest and money.* Atlantic Publishers.

Lawrence, P. R. and J. W. Lorsch. 1967. *Organization and Environment.* Homewood, IL: Irwin.

Lepper, M. R. and D. Greene. 1978. *The hidden costs of reward: New perspectives on the psychology of human motivation.* Hillsdale: Erlbaum.

Magidson, J. and A. E. Polcha. 1992. Creating market economics within companies. *Journal of Business Strategy* 13:39–44.

Malnight, T. W. 1996. The transition from decentralized to network-based MNC structures: An evolutionary perspective. *Journal of International Business Studies* 27:43–65.

Milgrom, P. and J. Roberts. 1992. *Economics, organization and management.* Englewood Cliffs, NJ: Prentice-Hall.

Mudambi, R. and P. Navarra. 2004. Is knowledge power? Knowledge flows, subsidiary power and rent-seeking within MNCs. *Journal of International Business Studies* 35:385–406.

Orton, J. D. and K. E. Weick. 1990. Loosely coupled systems: A reconceptualization. *Academy of Management Review* 15:203–23.

Osterloh, M. and B. S. Frey. 2000. Motivation, knowledge transfer, and organizational forms. *Organization Science* 11:538–50.

Prahalad, C. K. and Y. Doz. 1987. *The multinational mission: Balancing local demands and global vision.* New York: Free Press.

Qiu, J. X. and L. Donaldson. 2010. The cubic contingency model: Toward a more comprehensive international strategy-structure model. *Journal of General Management* 36:81–100.

Qiu, J. X. and L. Donaldson. 2012. Stopford and Wells were right! MNC matrix structures do fit a high-high strategy. *Management International Review* 52: 671–89.

Stopford, J. M. and L. T. Wells, Jr. 1972. *Managing the multinational enterprise.* New York: Basic Books.

Toyne, B. and R. J. Kuehne. 1983. The management of the international executive compensation and benefits process. *Journal of International Business Studies* 29:37–50.

Tushman, M. L. and D. A. Nadler. 1978. Information processing as an integrating concept in organizational design. *Academy of Management Review* 3:613–24.

White, R. E. and T. A. Poynter. 1990. Organizing for world-wide advantage. In *Managing the global firm.* Bartlett, C. A., Y. Doz, and G. Hedlund, eds. New York: Routledge.

Williamson, O. 1975. *Markets and hierarchies: Analysis and antitrust implications.* New York: Free Press.

Williamson, O. 1991. Comparative economic organization: The analysis of discrete structural alternatives. *Administrative Science Quarterly* 36:269–96.

Wolf, J. and W. G. Egelhoff. 2002. A re-examination and extension of international strategy-structure theory. *Strategic Management Journal* 23:181–89.

Youssef, S. M. 1975. Contextual factors influencing control strategy of multinational corporations. *Academy of Management Journal* 18:136–43.

7 "Managers to the Rescue!"

Evaluating the Legacy of
Stewardship Theory from an
Institutional Perspective

*Jaco Lok, Hokyu Hwang,
and Markus A. Höllerer*

The relationship between owners and managers—i.e., the question of corporate governance and control—has been a central concern of organization and management theory for many decades (Berle and Means 1932; Djelic 2013; Fiss 2008). Lex Donaldson's work (e.g., J. Davis, Schoorman, and Donaldson 1997; Donaldson and Davis 1991) on stewardship theory in the 1990s sparked an important and vibrant debate that continues to unfold today. Should management be governed by the principles of agency theory, which at its core assumes that the interests of managers, and those of the firm and its owners (and maybe society at large), are misaligned? Or should management be based on stewardship theory's central proposition that these interests are (or can be) intrinsically aligned? These questions reflect a key concern not only of scholars of organization and management but also of contemporary societies more broadly, as corporations increasingly wield power and influence over a broad range of societal domains (Perrow 1991).

The increasing transformation of traditional socioeconomic forms, such as state bureaucracies, professions, and civil society, into formalized and managed organizations has been a defining feature of modern societies (Drori, Höllerer, and Walgenbach 2014; Drori, Meyer, and Hwang 2006). Formal organization and practices of organizing have now expanded into virtually all societal domains (Bromley and Meyer 2016). Organization and management theory has been an invaluable intellectual endeavor in understanding this modern world of managed organizations (Scott and Davis 2006). While such a theory partly arises from observing and analyzing organizations and organizational life, its use—and usefulness—is not limited to mere descriptions and analyses of the empirical world of organizations. Precisely *because* organizations are purposively built collectivities and articulated formalizations of cultural beliefs, there is a performative aspect to organization and management theory in its entirety (Ferraro, Pfeffer, and Sutton 2005; MacKenzie 2008). That is, "organization and organization theory are visions as well as practices [. . .]. Organization theory drives the kinds of organizations that people build in the real world, and greatly affects the ways existing organizations change" (Meyer 2015, ix). Consequently, the question of which theories (should) dominate in scientific discourse and influence teaching in business schools and economics departments is by no means trivial.

In this chapter, we critically evaluate the legacy of Donaldson's conceptualization of stewardship theory in modern organization and management theory, highlighting its influential contributions to contemporary debates on the role of the corporation. Specifically, we review stewardship theory and its impact on our field in opposition to the dominant view of agency theory, and we analyze the broader historical context of this debate in a way that enables us to understand better stewardship theory's contemporary significance. We also offer some critical notes from an institutional perspective as a basis for arguing that stewardship theory's significance for contemporary debates on corporate governance and the role of the corporation does not necessarily lie in its ability to offer a more accurate, empirically falsifiable theory of managerial motivation than agency theory. Rather, it is important and relevant to contemporary debates on, for example, executive pay or the Global Financial Crisis, because it offers a platform for developing and considering new political alternatives to agency theory's dominance in shaping corporate governance practices. This dominance has produced very little except a self-fulfilling reaffirmation of its negative assumptions about the drivers of human behavior, against which stewardship theory can still act as an important counterpoint.

The Stewardship versus Agency Theory Debate as a Key Juncture in the Historical Trajectory of Modern Capitalism

Ideas on the "corporation," the relationship between owners, managers, and society at large, and, with this, the capitalist system in general, have not been stable over time. On the contrary, modern capitalism has followed a distinctive trajectory that has shaped, and was mutually shaped by, the theories that aimed to explain the socioeconomic world. As such, this history forms an important backdrop to the stewardship versus agency theory debate of the 1990s and is central to this chapter. This debate represented a key juncture in modern capitalism's historical trajectory in the Anglo-American economy and is still relevant, if not central, to recent attempts to reshape the corporation so that the pursuit of broader societal interests, rather than narrow short-term shareholder value maximization, becomes the guiding principle of the corporation. Next, we summarize this history as a way of highlighting the specific historical and institutional contingencies of the stewardship versus agency theory debate that informed it.

The Rise of Managerial Capitalism

In the history of the publicly owned corporation, the emergence of large (industrial) firms and the subsequent dispersion of corporate ownership in the late nineteenth and early twentieth centuries ushered in a new era in the development of capitalism—something that scholars have called "managerial capitalism" (G. Davis 2009; Khurana 2007; see also Perrow 1991). Corporations managed by a powerful and autonomous professional-managerial elite characterized this new form of capitalism. This new elite gradually replaced the role of owner-managers who were central to earlier capitalist forms. G. Davis (2009, 9) aptly describes managerial capitalism as a regime in which "corporate control was centripetal, accumulating in the hands of management, while ownership was centrifugal, becoming increasingly dispersed among thousands of anonymous (and powerless) stockholders." The resulting increase in the separation of ownership and control led to the fear that the concentration of power in the hands of professional managers, and the concurrent dispersion of ownership, would lead to the abusive use of managerial power and the uncontrolled pursuit of managers' self-interests.

This fear, however, did not quite materialize in reality—at least, not immediately. Corporations emerged not only as the dominant economic force but also as a social institution whose influence and reach extended well beyond the economic sphere by becoming the symbol of the productive and technological capacity of capitalism itself. As Peter Drucker put it, "The big enterprise is the true symbol of our social order [. . .]. In the industrial enterprise the structure which actually underlies all our society can be seen" (quoted in G. Davis 2009, 73). Ever larger organizations produced more levels of organizational hierarchy and, thus, more managerial opportunities as the power, prestige, and salaries of managers correlated with the size of the organization. This link between managerial salaries and organizational size meant that managerial interests became tightly aligned with the continued growth of the corporation. Consequently, managers primarily focused their efforts on sustaining and growing corporations rather than, for example, on profit maximization. Moreover, the increasing professionalization of management created "a commitment to the corporation itself as an institution endowed with responsibilities to employees, customers, communities, and other stakeholders [. . .], in short, *noblesse oblige*" (G. Davis 2009, 10). Thus the corporation was not simply an economic entity narrowly concerned with the financial welfare of its owners; rather, it had a broader reach and influence beyond its economic role. Its managers acted as the guardians of this societal institution, which infused the corporation with distinct values oriented at broad socioeconomic development and required the balancing of various stakeholder interests.

The Rise of Investor Capitalism

After the passage of the Celler-Kefauver Act of 1950 into law, which prevented the acquisitions of competing firms and suppliers, diversification into unrelated businesses became the predominant way of pursuing corporate growth in the United States. As a result, under managerial capitalism, large corporations became diversified conglomerates. Stiff foreign competition and the generally weak economic conditions in the early 1970s, however, precipitated a crisis in this growth strategy as corporations struggled to find profits in the harsher economic climate.

Shareholders began to accuse management of "empire building," i.e., growing for growth's sake in order to increase their own status and wealth rather than acting in the interest of shareholders. At the same time, the rising influence of the work of Milton Friedman and the Chicago School of Economics, coupled with the election of President Reagan, created the regulatory conditions for the emergence of a new market for corporate control in which publicly listed firms could be bought and sold more freely. If corporations were under-delivering and their share prices reflected poor performance, outsiders should be allowed to take over the underperforming firms and replace its management, thus unlocking the firm's true value potential. A market for corporate control, then, would benefit owners and firms alike by disciplining managers and thus realigning their interests with those of shareholders. The threat of a takeover, in addition, would force managers to divest unproductive businesses and concentrate on their core business, thereby releasing cash back to the shareholders through share buybacks and, consequently, reducing the supply of their stock (G. Davis, Diekmann, and Tinsley 1994; G. Davis and Stout 1992; Westphal and Zajac 2001).

As a result, corporate raiders began targeting diversified firms to "unlock" the hidden value that could be realized by breaking up conglomerates and selling off its parts. Institutional investors began to realize that they could benefit from such activity, thus further fueling a general movement of increased shareholder activism throughout the 1980s in both the United States and the United Kingdom. This movement gradually aligned the interests of institutional investors, corporate raiders, and hedge fund managers in opposition to those of management, who were accused of hanging on to their power at all costs and ignoring the rights of shareholders as the rightful owners of the corporation. In order to break this managerial power, the threat of takeover was increasingly seen as an effective mechanism for forcing management to pay more attention to the value they ought to create for shareholders. In this way, managerial capitalism shifted to what commentators have labeled as a shift toward "investor capitalism" (Useem 1996) and the associated shareholder value conception of corporate control (G. Davis and Thompson 1994; Fligstein 2001; Zorn, Dobbin, Dierkes, and Kwok 2004). According to this new institutional logic, the sole purpose of management was to maximize shareholder value in the interest of the corporation's owners. Thus changing conceptions of control reshaped the primary orientation of the corporation and its management as one of the dominant actor forms in contemporary society.

The Role of Agency Theory in the Rise of Investor Capitalism

Providing the intellectual arsenal and ammunition for this new conception of the corporation and the role of management was agency theory. Developed in the late 1970s and throughout the 1980s by finance theorists, agency theory reflected and fueled the struggle of shareholders in the United States, and later the United Kingdom, to increase their control over management by complementing a persuasive diagnosis of the problem of managerial capitalism with an equally compelling solution. As an economic theory of social exchange rooted in *homo economicus* assumptions of human behavior, it conceptualized the corporation as a "nexus of treaties," with shareholders depicted as its owners, or "principals," and management as their "agents" (Jensen and Meckling 1976). According to agency theory, the key issue with managerial capitalism was the "principal-agent problem": agents—management—could reasonably be expected to shirk from their responsibility to act in the interest of their principals—shareholders—when they benefited from asymmetric information that could be (ab)used to serve their own self-interests rather than those of shareholders as the rightful owners of the corporation. The economic problems of the 1970s could thus be explained based on a fundamental misalignment of the interests of shareholders (and through them, the economy at large) and those of managers, who were seen to have hijacked the corporation for their own self-interested purposes.

In order to solve this problem, managers needed to be incentivized to act in the sole interest of shareholders, thus ensuring that they would not waste resources on projects that were not directly contributing to the ultimate objective of shareholder value maximization. In order for a free market for corporate control to act as a disciplinary mechanism toward this purpose, agency theorists focused on devising managerial incentive schemes to ensure that managerial interests were aligned with those of the shareholders by rewarding management as if they were owners. Thus stock options were pushed as the primary method for compensating executives, because they could ensure that the management would focus exclusively on shareholder value maximization in order to boost their own pay through the stock options they were awarded. For example, in an influential *Harvard Business Review* article in 1990, Jensen and Murphy argued that the problem was that executives were paid like "bureaucrats" and called for big rewards for superior performance and big penalties for poor performance. As a result of this push, stock options came to represent more than half of the pay packages of Fortune 500 CEOs in the United States by 2001, which was up from less than a quarter in 1992.

Alongside this development, CEO turnover rates increased significantly as a result of a tighter link between CEO tenure and stock performance based on the increasing willingness on the part of shareholders to force the board to replace management if and when they underperformed the market. The average tenure of a Fortune 500 CEO steadily declined to less than five years by 2010, which is a trend that was mirrored in the United Kingdom. As a result of the combined effects of the increased threat of takeover through the market for corporate control, the increased rewards for superior stock price performance in the form of stock options, and the increased threat of being fired for underperformance, managers gradually adopted their newly defined role as agents in the service of shareholders, despite the loss of power this necessarily entailed. Whereas in the 1980s it was not uncommon for CEOs to publicly distance themselves from analysts and the share price by claiming that the financial markets could not possibly accurately reflect what went on inside their company, such critical voices gradually disappeared as any CEO who was not seen to be acting in the interest of shareholder value maximization would quickly find him/herself out of the job.

By reframing and restricting management's role to agents in the sole service of shareholders as their principals, the shareholder value movement and its specific brand of investor capitalism succeeded in significantly decreasing managerial power in the United States and United Kingdom. Agency theory provided both ideological and theoretical rationales for the corporate control and governance practices that dominated much of the late twentieth century, thus directly contributing to the relative decline of managerialism, at least in the corporate sectors of the United States and United Kingdom (Khurana 2007). With the globalization of corporate finance and the increasing interest of activist US institutional investors in European stocks, shareholder value thinking also began to spread into continental Europe, although its effects were less pronounced there due to important legal and institutional differences that buffered European corporations from the rise of the more aggressive forms of investor capitalism (Fiss and Zajac 2004; Meyer and Höllerer 2010). Yet, in line with global trends, CEO pay packages in Western Europe also significantly increased as average CEO tenure continued to decrease, reflecting an increasing willingness on the part of shareholders to exercise their power more broadly to discipline top management through a combination of financial incentives and the threat of forcing the board to replace them when they underperformed the market.

Stewardship Theory's Legacy as a Counterweight to Agency Theory-Based Corporate Governance

At the very height of agency theory's popularity, and in the midst of the associated shift from managerial to investor capitalism in the United States and the United Kingdom, Donaldson and Davis (1991) published their caution "against too ready acceptance of the agency theory model of CEO role and rewards" (Donaldson and Davis 1991, 50). They pointed out that agency theory's "model of man" as a self-interested actor who rationally optimized his own personal economic gain showed a strong resemblance to McGregor's (1960) Theory X. In contrast, they argued that managerial role holders could actually be intrinsically motivated by performing challenging work, exercising responsibility and authority, and gaining recognition from peers. Moreover, long tenure could lead to managers identifying with the corporation, thus "melding individual self-esteem with corporate prestige" (Donaldson and Davis 1991, 51). The promise of future employment and pension rights could also be sufficient to ensure that their self-perceived interests are aligned with the corporation and its owners, without the need for stock options.

Thus, in direct contradiction to agency theory, stewardship theory held that "there is no inherent, general problem of executive motivation" (Donaldson and Davis 1991, 51). Moreover, it also directly opposed corporate governance policies of the United States and United Kingdom that advocated a strict separation between the CEO role and the chairman of the board in order to ensure adequate independent disciplinary oversight of management's activities. Instead, Donaldson and Davis radically recommended that "the CEO exercises complete authority over the corporation and that their role is unambiguous and unchallenged" (Donaldson and Davis 1991, 52), thus suggesting that the CEO and chairman roles should be combined. In their 1997 paper on stewardship theory in the *Academy of Management Review*, J. Davis, Schoorman, and Donaldson repeated this prescription:

> A steward's autonomy should be deliberately extended to maximize the benefits of a steward, because he or she can be trusted [. . .]. Indeed, control can be potentially counterproductive, because it undermines that pro-organizational behavior of the steward, by lowering his or her motivation.
>
> (J. Davis et al. 1997, 25)

They also reasserted the superiority of stewardship theory by arguing that it offered the "highest joint utility" (J. Davis et al. 1997, 40) for both management and shareholders, in addition to offering a more accurate description of managerial motivations. Yet, at the same time, they also refined the clear opposition of early stewardship theory to agency theory by suggesting that psychological and situational factors could predispose some managers to behave as stewards and others as self-interested agents. This more contingent, situational perspective led them to predict that both shareholders and management would most likely opt to behave according to a principal-agent relationship, instead of a mutual stewardship relationship, because the perceived costs of betrayal by the other party are higher than the perceived collective gains of enacting a mutual stewardship relationship. Hence their implicit explanation for the continued rise of investor capitalism based on principal-agent thinking throughout the 1980s and 1990s was that both shareholders and management were locked in a prisoner's dilemma, despite management's inherent trustworthiness under specific psychological and situational conditions.

By pointing to a clear possible alternative to corporate governance policies based on agency theory assumptions, Donaldson's stewardship theory radically flew against the relentless institutional trend toward building governance safeguards and incentive schemes that were oriented at containing management's presumed tendencies to act in their own self-interest. As such, stewardship theory formed a critical juncture in the trajectory of modern capitalism by pointing to a possible alternative way for organizing the relationships between the corporation, management, and shareholders. Yet, as Davis et al. (1997) predicted, this alternative was never realized, as corporate governance committees and regulators in both the United States and United Kingdom continued to design risk-averse corporate governance policies that were based on agency theory assumptions and therefore oriented at minimizing the probability of managerial shirking:

> Risk-averse owners will most likely perceive that executives are self-serving and will prefer agency governance prescriptions. Implementing stewardship governance mechanisms for an agent would be analogous to turning the hen house over to the fox. Agency prescriptions can be viewed as the necessary costs of insuring principal utility against the risks of executive opportunism. From this perspective, a better question might be: Why would an owner ever take the risks of stewardship governance prescriptions?
>
> (J. Davis et al. 1997, 26)

Meanwhile, as average CEO tenure steadily declined because of increased shareholder willingness to replace management, the perceived risk of taking up a senior management position therefore increased, prompting top management teams to protect both their potential upside (through stock options) as well as their downside (through negotiating lucrative golden parachutes). Such behavior was, of course, seen by agency theory proponents as yet another confirmation of management's tendency to act in a purely self-interested way by opportunistically grabbing a disproportionate share of company assets for personal gain when given the chance. As pressures on management for continued short-term strong financial performance increased through constantly greater rewards for strong performance, as well as through more immediate penalties for poor performance, the number of large corporate scandals also increased, providing yet more supposed evidence for the agency theory thesis. From this perspective, Donaldson and colleagues must clearly be wrong, because over the past 20 years, top management has given us very little indication that they are willing to act as responsible stewards. Instead, both the finance industry and top management now face a serious societal legitimacy challenge based on their perceived "fat cat," opportunistic, money-grabbing behavior and their blatant disregard for the collective consequences of their narcissism.

Yet, despite this seemingly overwhelming evidence of top management's self-interested behavior over the past 20 years, J. Davis et al. (1997) hinted at a possible explanation for such behavior that was radically different from agency theory. Rather than objective evidence of management's true self-interested motivations, their behavior in the form of increased pay demands and increased cheating may have been a *self-fulfilling outcome* of the very theory of man on which agency theory and the corporate governance policies and incentive schemes it informed were based:

> When stewards are controlled as if they were agents, they cannot enjoy the types of internal rewards they desire (i.e., growth, achievement, or self-actualization), and as a result, they may engage in antiorganizational behaviors. (. . .) Managers in controlling, less trusting climates may not have the opportunity to behave as stewards and therefore may experience decreased feelings of self-worth, self-responsibility, and self-control and have less desire to behave as stewards. (. . .) In such environments, [they] may resort to antagonistic adaptive activities such as (. . .) demanding better financial compensation [and] benefits.
>
> (J. Davis et al. 1997, 39–40)

Thus one of the important legacies of Donaldson's stewardship theory is that it implicitly offers a radically different thesis for the reason investor capitalism finds itself in such trouble today: it has become the victim of its own underlying assumptions regarding human motivation, which have become self-fulfilling through an exclusive mutual focus on risk control on the part of shareholders and management. Therefore, rather than offering proof of the nature of management's "true" motivations, their apparent self-interested behavior may be nothing but a rational consequence of continuing to treat themselves *as if* they were self-interested agents. Moreover, not only does stewardship offer the potential for this radically different understanding of the root cause of investor capitalism's current legitimacy crisis, it also still offers a possible *alternative to* investor capitalism by pointing to the possibility, and need, for a more collective orientation toward the potential gain of creating the structural conditions under which stewardship behavior becomes possible. Given the current dire state of investor capitalism, it may well be worth exploring this possibility more seriously today. As such, stewardship theory has not lost any of its contemporary relevance.

Despite its continued relevance, however, for stewardship theory's potential to act as the basis for the realization of an alternative to the negative excesses of investor capitalism, clearly a lot of hard work would still need to be carried out. To start with, its thesis that management is inherently trustworthy if given the chance will be extremely difficult to sell to both regulators and shareholders who have, for several decades, focused their efforts squarely on containing a range of managerial behaviors that appear to come to the exact opposite conclusion. When one is faced with a perceived threat from another party, who also feels threatened by one's presence, one can either opt to protect oneself by assuming the worst, or seek to reassure the other party that they should not feel threatened in the hope that they may behave in good faith in return. In the 1990s in Northern Ireland, to provide a more general example, we saw how the latter strategy was pursued to address a long-term and entrenched conflict. By carefully repairing minimally sufficient trust on both sides to allow for new governance relations, through which mutually perceived risks could be significantly reduced, superior collective outcomes at the state level were created. In contrast, the Middle East peace accord reached by Rabin, Arafat, and Clinton in the mid-1990s was fatally undermined by radical elements on both sides pursuing the more risk-averse, self-protective strategy. Despite the accord's new collective orientation toward more productive relations based on mutual assurances of good faith and the promise of peace, key groups refused to believe that those on the other side could ever be trusted and sought to protect their sectional political interests by maintaining the status quo through their continued opposition to the peace accord instead of seeing it as a unique opportunity to reorient their behavior toward the collectively superior outcome of peace. Hence the continued practical relevance of stewardship theory may hinge on the possibility of rebuilding a minimum level of trustworthiness of managers in the eyes of shareholders, regulators, and the general public. This will, of course, prove difficult in a corporate governance system that produces the very managerial motivations it aims to compensate against.

Yet a new institutional opportunity structure may currently be emerging through which more productive corporate governance relations based on stewardship theory may yet become feasible. At societal level, the problems and excesses of unbridled investor capitalism have not gone unnoticed. Indeed, in the United Kingdom, for example, a series of different corporate governance codes have sought to address and combat a number of negative consequences of the shareholder value maximization logic, including, but not limited to, short-termism, fraud, excessive executive pay, and neglect of the interests of other stakeholders such as employees, the community, and the natural environment. This approach has tried to soften some of investor capitalism's sharper edges by recasting it under the rubric of *"enlightened* shareholder value" under which *both* investors *and* management were expected to act responsibly beyond a sole concern for short-term financial gain (Lok 2010). At the same time, notions of corporate social responsibility (CSR) and corporate sustainability (e.g., Höllerer 2013; Matten and Moon 2008) have become increasingly prevalent in modern-day corporations, including the argument that these practices may actually enhance shareholder value in the long run.

These trends are increasingly referred to under the rubric of a general move from investor capitalism toward "responsible capitalism." The preferred way to enforce such increased responsibility still appears to be to rely on institutional investors to pressure management into more responsible decision making, thus preserving the principal-agent divide. This appears to neglect the fact that many institutional investors are not actually in a good position to enforce greater corporate responsibility because of their fiduciary obligation to maximize financial returns for their investees. This obligation has led to organizational structures and practices that do not really enable them to act as "responsible owners" (Lok 2010). Yet the move toward considering the interests and concerns of a broader set of stakeholders than just shareholder value maximization alone appears bound to reinstate some of management's relative power vis-à-vis shareholders. After all, only management is in a position to adequately understand and balance different stakeholder needs in relation to the overall objective of shareholder value maximization. A general move toward responsible capitalism could, therefore, offer a new set of institutional conditions under which the practical implications of stewardship theory for corporate governance may be reconsidered. This becomes particularly evident when, for example, taking into account the recent commentary emphasizing the *individual-level* responsibility of managers, which goes beyond an abstract organization-level CSR or "enlightened" orientation.

Any fundamental rethinking of managerial responsibility in relation to "responsible capitalism" is bound to lead to a review of current managerial incentive schemes and disciplinary mechanisms. This is precisely because these are based on agency theory assumptions that are not oriented toward promoting and incentivizing the type of stewardship that would be required under responsible capitalism. The legacy of Donaldson's work on stewardship theory, therefore, is that as a precursor to the current emerging debate within organization and management theory on responsible capitalism, it has opened up a discursive space for considering alternatives to corporate governance systems that are solely based on agency theory assumptions. This legacy may still pave the way for a broad academic and societal debate through which the current system of corporate governance can be reimagined.

Critical Notes on Stewardship Theory Based on an Institutional Theory Perspective

From the earlier analysis of stewardship's legacy and its contemporary relevance, it should be clear that we see Donaldson's intervention as part and parcel of a more general, normative political debate on the responsibilities of the corporation and management in relation to shareholders and other stakeholders. This debate has been ongoing ever since the birth of the public corporation hundreds of years ago. From this institutional perspective, shifts from one form of capitalism to another necessarily involve shifts in power relations that are constituted in the rationale, practice prescriptions, and associated role identities—or institutional logic—on which a particular new form of capitalism is based. The shift from managerial capitalism to investor capitalism involved a clear shift in power from management toward shareholders based on the new principal-agent role identities that were assigned to them (Lok 2010). From this perspective, it is no coincidence that agency theory, which promoted the rights of shareholders to exert more power over management, was developed in finance departments. Likewise, it is no surprise that its rise in both practice and scholarship provoked a reaction from management departments in the form of Donaldson's stewardship theory. After all, stewardship theory offered a theoretical and practical alternative through which managerial power could be preserved vis-à-vis shareholders by (re-)legitimating management's ultimate control over the corporation and, with it, the legitimacy of management departments to speak on their behalf.

In this way, the academic debate between agency theory and stewardship theory not only reflected, but actually formed, an integral part of a broader political struggle between shareholders and management over whose conception of control of the corporation would prevail (Fligstein 1991). This struggle not only continues to play itself out in corporate boardrooms, but it also revolves around different academic departments that are able to legitimate different institutional regimes through the theories they produce. The rise of the specific power regime that a particular academic discipline represents and advocates usually goes together with the rise of its voice and dominance in academic debates, including the associated academic status markers that come with such dominance in the form of the holy grail of "academic impact" based on citation rates. It is interesting to note in this regard that although J. Davis, Schoorman, and Donaldson's (1997) article on stewardship theory has clearly been impactful as evidenced by more than three thousand Google Scholar citations, this citation rate pales into insignificance compared to Jensen and Meckling's (1976) foundational article on agency theory, which has more than 56,500 citations—nearly 20 times as much. From this comparative academic impact perspective, stewardship theory can be seen as a belated, and relatively unsuccessful, attempt to wrestle academic and practice dominance away from agency theorists.

Yet neither agency theory nor stewardship theory is ever reflexively presented in this politicized way; their designers are seemingly happy to have their theories used by practitioners to support and legitimate their specific political agendas, while claiming to have no stake in the resulting political struggles themselves. Indeed, the political power of these theories actually resides in their claims to scientific objectivity and falsifiability, because it is only through this apparent political neutrality that their relative ability to legitimate one form of corporate governance over another is able to take on the serious weight of "scientific truth": if agency theory is correct, then its prescriptions should be accepted; if stewardship theory is correct, then an alternative corporate governance system ought to be developed. Yet this seductively beautiful simplicity of using scientific research to decide which theory is correct, as a basis for designing corporate governance systems that maximize societal utility, belies the fact that such research becomes impossible when the theories that are to be compared and tested shape the very empirical domain to which they apply. Stewardship theory went as far as to acknowledge this implicitly—at least in the case of agency theory—by arguing that agency theory may well be self-fulfilling: *creating* the very empirical conditions that would invoke behaviors that could be used to scientifically confirm its original assumptions. Indeed, we see this insight as one of stewardship theory's key strengths, because it enables us to consider current institutional arrangements and associated behaviors as less than inevitable and therefore open to change for the better.

Yet, despite this implicit acknowledgment of what Giddens (1984) refers to as the "double hermeneutic" in the case of agency theory, stewardship theory still presented *its own* propositions regarding the manager and his/her motivations as evidently universal and falsifiable. Such positivistic framing neglects the possibility that what and who managers "are," how they are motivated, and how they behave is always going to be historically and institutionally contingent—that is, embedded in dominant cultural belief systems that are supported by scientific discourses, including stewardship theory, that actively *construct* them. Thus one of the fundamental insights and possible contributions of institutional thinking to the agency versus stewardship theory debate is that what "the manager" is (or ought to be) is socially constructed and therefore culturally and historically contingent. According to this perspective, there is no reason to believe that the manager's "true" motivations ought to remain stable over time and can ever be "discovered" or empirically "verified" as universally valid under specific situational and psychological conditions. This is because what he or she is, ought to do, and ought to feel changes over time as a partial result of the very theories that aim to capture and explain them. Both agency theory and stewardship theory, therefore, not only *reflect* the broader political struggle between shareholders and management for corporate control that has played itself out over the past three decades, but they can also be seen as *affecting* and *effecting* this very struggle.

The implication of this key institutional argument is that we will not ever be able to settle the agency versus stewardship theory debate by developing increasingly intricate psychological and situational boundary conditions under which each can be empirically shown to be more predictive of managerial motivations and behavior. Indeed, as societal conceptions of control of the firm continue to shift over time, different managerial classes rise to power with different value orientations, motivations, and strategic decision-making heuristics (Fligstein 1991). In other words, the managers that lead today's corporations are not the same as the stewards that acted as the corporation's guardians under managerial capitalism, because their role identities are embedded in a completely different institutional logic, regardless of the specific psychological and situational conditions—highlighted by J. Davis et al. (1997)—that may also inform them. The debate over which logic ought to be preferred as a basis for organizing the relations between the corporation, management, shareholders, and other stakeholders can therefore never be an exclusively scientific empirical question. Rather, it requires a *politico-ethical* debate in which social scientists could play an important role not only by being clear on the empirical boundary conditions of their theories but, more importantly, by also being more open and reflexive about the possible political and behavioral consequences of their theories if they were to be implemented.

We believe stewardship theory still has an important role to play in such a debate—not necessarily because it offers a more accurate theory of managerial motivation and behavior, but because it points to the political possibility of collectively reorienting the relationship between shareholders and management toward a broader societal purpose than self-interest alone. As such, it continues to offer an important counterweight to agency theory's rather depressing conclusion that the only way to orient management's behavior to act in line with interests other than those that merely serve themselves is to offer them carrots and sticks that are large enough to influence their behavior. Stewardship theory offers some hope that "responsible capitalism" may be more than a pipe dream as long as we can tap into other sources of motivation by fundamentally reimagining and reconstructing the role identities of both shareholders and management toward broader societal value creation. This, we believe, is the main challenge that lies before us today, as societies continue to search for viable alternatives to the excesses of unbridled investor capitalism.

In closing, we wish to express our appreciation for having had the privilege to participate in numerous scholarly conversations and debates with our UNSW colleague Lex Donaldson. His analysis of business organizations has always been true to his deep-felt beliefs, values, and academic standards; based on a solid line of argument; and always delivered in an eloquent, clear, and pointed manner. While we regularly "agreed to disagree" in our views on organization theory based on the divergent intellectual heritages we represent, we equally developed mutual respect for our different scholarly positions and certainly benefited greatly from these intellectual encounters. Lex's great intellectual curiosity, incredibly sharp mind, and respectful engagement with divergent arguments and views will continue to offer us a role model for how intellectual debate can be encouraged to the benefit of all who choose to participate in it.

References

Berle, A. A. and G. C. Means. 1932. *The modern corporation and private property.* New York: Macmillan.

Bromley, P. and J. W. Meyer. 2016. *Hyper-organization.* Oxford: Oxford University Press.

Davis, G. F. 2009. *Managed by the markets: How finance re-shaped America.* Oxford: Oxford University Press.

Davis, G. F., K. A. Diekmann, and C. H. Tinsley. 1994. The decline and fall of the conglomerate firm in the 1980s: The deinstitutionalization of an organizational form. *American Sociological Review* 59:547–70.

Davis, G. F. and S. K. Stout. 1992. Organization theory and the market for corporate control: A dynamic analysis of the characteristics of large takeover targets, 1980–1990. *Administrative Science Quarterly* 37:605–33.

Davis, G. F. and T. A. Thompson. 1994. A social movement perspective on corporate control. *Administrative Science Quarterly* 39:141–73.

Davis, J. H., F. D. Schoorman, and L. Donaldson. 1997. Toward a stewardship theory of management. *Academy of Management Review* 22:20–47.

Djelic, M.-L. 2013. When limited liability was (still) an issue: Mobilization and politics of signification in 19th-century England. *Organization Studies* 34:595–621.

Donaldson, L. and J. H. Davis. 1991. Stewardship theory or agency theory: CEO governance and shareholder returns. *Australian Journal of Management* 16:49–64.

Drori, G. S., M. A. Höllerer, and P. Walgenbach, eds. 2014. *Global themes and local variations in organizations and management: Perspectives on glocalization.* New York: Routledge.

Drori, G. S., J. W. Meyer, and H. Hwang, eds. 2006. *Globalization and organization: World society and organizational change.* Oxford: Oxford University Press.

Ferraro, F., J. Pfeffer, and R. I. Sutton. 2005. Economics language and assumptions: How theories can become self-fulfilling. *Academy of Management Review* 30:8–24.

Fiss, P. C. 2008. Institutions and corporate governance. In *The SAGE handbook of organizational institutionalism.* Greenwood, R., C. Oliver, K. Sahlin, and R. Suddaby, eds. London: Sage Publications, 389–410.

Fiss, P. C. and E. J. Zajac. 2004. The diffusion of ideas over contested terrain: The (non)adoption of a shareholder value orientation among German firms. *Administrative Science Quarterly* 49:501–34.

Fligstein, N. 1991. *The transformation of corporate control.* Cambridge: Harvard University Press.

Fligstein, N. 2001. Social skills and the theory of fields. *Sociological Theory* 19:105–25.

Giddens, A. 1984. *The constitution of society: Outline of the theory of structuration.* Berkeley and Los Angeles: University of California Press.

Höllerer, M. A. 2013. From taken-for-granted to explicit commitment: The rise of CSR in a corporatist country. *Journal of Management Studies* 50:573–606.

Jensen, M. C. and W. H. Meckling. 1976. Theory of the firm: Managerial behavior, agency costs and ownership structure. *Journal of Financial Economics* 3:305–60.

Jensen, M. C. and K. J. Murphy. 1990. CEO incentives: It's not how much you pay, but how. *Harvard Business Review* 68:138–53.

Khurana, R. 2007. *From higher aims to hired hands: The social transformation of American business schools and the unfulfilled promise of management as a profession.* Princeton: Princeton University Press.

Lok, J. 2010. Institutional logics as identity projects. *Academy of Management Journal* 53:1305–35.

MacKenzie, D. 2008. *An engine, not a camera: How financial models shape markets.* Cambridge: MIT Press.

Matten, D. and J. Moon. 2008. "Implicit" and "explicit" CSR: A conceptual framework for a comparative understanding of corporate social responsibility. *Academy of Management Review* 33:404–24.

McGregor, D. 1960. *The human side of enterprise.* New York: McGraw-Hill.

Meyer, J. W. 2015. Foreword. In *Classics of organization theory.* Shafritz, J. M., J. S. Ott, and Y. S. Jan, eds. Belmont: Wadsworth Publishing, ix–xii.

Meyer, R. E. and M. A. Höllerer. 2010. Meaning structures in a contested issue field: A topographic map of shareholder value in Austria. *Academy of Management Journal* 53:1241–62.

Perrow, C. 1991. A society of organizations. *Theory and Society* 20:725–62.

Scott, W. R. and G. F. Davis. 2006. *Organizations and organizing: Rational, natural and open system perspectives.* Upper Saddle River, NJ: Pearson Prentice-Hall.

Useem, M. 1996. *Investor capitalism: How money managers are changing the face of corporate America.* New York: Basic Books.

Westphal, J. D. and E. J. Zajac. 2001. Decoupling policy from practice: The case of stock repurchase programs. *Administrative Science Quarterly* 46:202–28.

Zorn, D., F. Dobbin, J. Dierkes, and M. Kwok. 2004. Managing investors: How financial markets reshaped the American firm. In *The sociology of financial markets.* Cetina, K. K. and A. Preda, eds. London: Oxford University Press, 269–89.

8 Conclusion

Lex Donaldson

Organizational theory research is flourishing. Organizational theory research covers a variety of topics and employs numerous theoretical approaches. Within this diversity, there is a need for some parts of the discourse to be focused to fully reap its insights so that some organization theory research is conducted within a particular paradigm. The chapters in this book are weighted toward research undertaken in the contingency theory paradigm (Donaldson 2001) and to a lesser degree the stewardship theory paradigm (Davis, Schoorman, and Donaldson 1997). They show that these two established traditions continue to have growth and relevance.

Some organizational structure research takes the contingency theory approach. It finds that the optimal organizational structure varies according to contingency factors so that to have high performance, the structure of the organization needs to fit the contingencies (Lawrence and Lorsch 1967). In the present book, Burton, Obel, and Håkonsson (chapter 1) offer a contingency model of contracting theory. This extends their program of reintegrating organizational theory by expressing each organizational theory as a contingency and then bringing the organizational theories together within a contingency framework. Klaas and Lauridsen (chapter 2) offer an analysis of the relationship between misfits and complexity.

Antithetically, some scholars have argued that there is no or little imperative to fit to contingencies, because multiple fits are available, that is, there is equifinality and strategic choice (Doty, Glick, and Huber 1993). However, Luo, Donaldson, and Yu show in this book (chapter 3) that equifinality seldom exists, whereas the contingency imperative idea largely holds true, thereby defending a central plank of contingency theory.

Binns and Tushman (chapter 4) tackle the important topic of innovation in the corporation. They find that success requires the adoption of an ambidexterity approach, whereby the processes of exploration and exploitation are separated out into distinct parts of the organization, allowing each structure to fit its different process.

The analysis of matrix structures by Qiu and Donaldson (chapter 5) probes the issue of whether MNC matrix structures, with their multidimensional organizational structures, are advantageous relative to simpler, single-dimensional organizational structures. It draws on the contingency fit idea as part of the prediction of the advantage of the matrix structure.

The contingency approach can also be used to combine theories in synthesis. Using the contingency idea at a more abstract and general level, Egelhoff and Wolf (chapter 6) argue that the way out of the fragmentation of contemporary organizational theory is to take the contingency approach and integrate research by finding the contingencies under which different organizational theories each hold true.

Turning to stewardship theory, and taking a sociological perspective, Lok, Hwang, and Höllerer (chapter 7) argue that stewardship theory would be more fruitful if combined with another theory—responsible capitalism—so that stewardship theory provided the micro foundations of responsible capitalism.

Many of the chapters in this book push forward with defending or extending contingency theory. Other chapters point the way forward for the wider contingency approach, as a means of achieving theoretical integration of organizational theories, or call for a synthesis of contingency theory with other sociological theories. In their various ways, the chapters in the present book suggest fresh research that may be undertaken in the future.

As the contingency theory of organizations has developed over time, more contingency factors or variables and their fitting structures have been identified. This poses a problem for those working within the contingency theory paradigm: how do the multiple contingency factors come together to determine the fitting structure for an organization? A major step forward has been the multiple-contingency model of Burton, Obel and their colleagues. They have constructed a model in which numerous contingency factors jointly define the fit for an organization (Burton and Obel 1998). In this way, arguments that fit is determined by strategy, size and so on, are accommodated. Prescriptions are offered in the form of structural and other variables whose levels fit the levels of the multiple contingencies (and this has been made available as a computer model). This eclectic synthesis has not to date included the ideas of transaction cost theory. In their chapter (chapter 1), Burton et al. seek to integrate transaction costs theory into their model of multiple contingencies of organization.

Transaction costs theory holds that while markets are effective in some conditions, in other conditions, hierarchy is more effective (Williamson 1975). The theory specifies the nature of these conditions, such as asset specific investment. In contingency theory terms, market transactions fit lack of asset specific investments while hierarchical structures fit asset specific investments (and so on, for other conditioning factors). Thus the theory states a set of contingency factors that determine which organizational structures are most effective and thereby the theory states the fits of contracts to contingencies. In this way, transaction costs theory can have a broadly similar underlying theoretical structure to contingency theory.

Burton, Obel, and Håkonsson argue that the transaction costs approach is complementary to the preceding approaches about organizational design.

They display this by considering the various forms of contracting in transaction costs theory, distinguishing between formal contracting on the one hand and agile and relational contracting on the other hand. These different types of contracting each fit different levels of uncertainty, so that uncertainty plays the role of a contingency factor (similarly for asset specific investments).

There is an added subtlety that, for Burton et al., formal contracting tends to reduce the uncertainty of a transaction. Thus the causal relationship between uncertainty and formal contracting is two-way: uncertainty reduces the formality of contracting and the formality of contracting reduces the uncertainty of contracting. But, it should be noted that, whereas the effect of contracting on uncertainty is direct (i.e., contracting reduces uncertainty), the effect of uncertainty on contracting formality would be indirect. This is because the effect of uncertainty on contracting goes via fit. Uncertainty would lead to agile and relational contracting only after formal contracting, which misfits uncertainty, has led to lower performance. Then an adaptive change is made by adopting either agile or relational contracting and thereby regaining fit and performance. At the least, this would be the causal process connecting uncertainty and contracting according to the SARFIT model of organizational change, i.e., Structural Adaptation to Regain Fit (Donaldson 2001).

The idea of contracting being a new structural factor that fits some contingency factors within the over-arching theoretical syntheses of Burton et al., is to be welcomed. However, as we just saw, those pursuing contracting as a contingency in future research will need to be careful to specify the time ordering of variables, such as contracting formality and uncertainty, stating which is the cause and which is the effect. Future researchers should also specify whether each causal relationship is direct, or indirect by passing through misfit and fit of contracting to the contingency variables. In this way, the validity of the contingency model of contracting may be ascertained. The contracting perspective may then take its proper place in the existing multiple-contingency model of organizational design of Burton et al., which offers valuable guidance for managers, directors and consultants.

The chapter by Klaas and Lauridsen continues the contingency theory theme, dealing as it does with misfits of the structures to the contingencies. Whereas traditionally contingency theory research tends to focus on a single misfit and how it is turned into a fit, Klaas and Lauridsen discuss multiple misfits of structures to contingencies. They explore the interactions, or lack thereof, between misfits. One of the ideas they deal with is that fixing one misfit by changing it to a fit could turn numerous other fits into misfits, so that the benefit from creating the first fit could be over-shadowed by the disadvantages from creating the new misfits. This has led some to argue that incremental change by correcting one or two misfits at a time is actually detrimental to organizational performance, so that revolutionary change is preferable, leading to performance improvements. However, Klaas and

Lauridsen find empirically that incremental change produces more beneficial outcomes than revolutionary change.

The method of Klaas and Lauridsen is somewhat novel and unusual (though following the stream of research of Burton, Obel, and colleagues). They consider many more fits and misfits between more structures and their contingencies than is customary in contingency theory research. The repercussions of changing misfits to fits in terms of the new fits and misfits produced are identified. Notably, the misfits compared with fits are ascertained for the whole set of structures and contingencies. The patterns formed are compared with statistical distributions. These results are then used to distinguish between the likely underlying processes, such as organizational complexity. This macroscopic analysis of fits and misfits is a potentially major advance in organizational theory research, most especially when it is tied back to theory, such as complexity theory. Future research could well use more of this approach of analyzing together the fits and misfits between the many structures and contingencies that have been identified over the years by contingency theory research.

The chapter by Luo et al. (chapter 3) raises one of the most controversial questions in contingency theory: strategic choice. The original structural contingency theory held that contingency factors determined organizational structure, because organizations adapted to avoid loss of performance (Burns and Stalker 1961). "Strategic choice" (Child 1972)—which would be more clearly termed structural choice (see Donaldson 1996)—challenged that determinism and argued that there was a choice of structures. A major argument for strategic choice was that, rather than there being one structure that fitted the contingencies, there was a range of structures that fitted the contingencies. Thereby there was a choice of structures that could avoid performance loss. The idea that multiple structures could produce the same high-performance levels is known as equifinality. Equifinality has become a popular idea (Child 1977, 1984; Gresov and Drazin 1997), but, as Luo et al. argue in their chapter, it is most unlikely to occur in practice for three reasons. First, as Luo et al. argue, equifinality only exists where contingencies conflict by each requiring a different level of the same structural variable. Yet it is possible for contingencies to be consistent. Then the fitting level of structure for one contingency is also the fitting level of structure for the other contingency. This means there are no different structures that are equally effective, and so no equifinality.

Second, where contingencies are inconsistent in the structures they require, this is only equifinality if the importance of the contingencies are equal. Otherwise, the fitting structure is the one with the greatest impact. Equifinality assumes that the fits of structures to contingencies have the same amount of effect on organizational performance, yet that lacks a basis in theory and empirical evidence (see Luo et al., chapter 3 this volume). Third, even where the first two objections to equifinality do not hold, equifinality can still be avoided through structural separation. Conflicting structures created by different contingencies may be dealt with by having the different structures that they require each be housed in a different part of the organization. (This is the structural ambidexterity discussed by Binns and Tushman in their chapter.)

Only if these three objections all fail will equifinality apply in an organization, thus opening the door to the possibility of strategic choice (though other impediments to strategic choice also exist; see Donaldson 1996).

As equifinality is unlikely in practice, the argument for strategic choice that relies on equifinality will seldom hold true. An organization seeking to avoid performance loss will need to adopt the structure that best fits its contingencies. Hence there will normally be a contingency imperative: the organization must bow to the dictates of contingencies or suffer loss of performance. This was the message of the original structural contingency theory. Equifinality (and strategic choice) is a modification to contingency theory that contradicts its basic point. Thus the critique of equifinality presented in this book is a call for a return to a stronger, less internally conflicted, form of contingency theory.

Although some organization theory scholars have sought to refute or minimize the idea of a contingency imperative by arguing for equifinality, and hence strategic choice, Luo et al., have herein presented an argument against equifinality. However, the argumentation is somewhat abstract and skeletal. There is room for future research to examine their arguments critically and to put them to the test theoretically and empirically. Are the theoretical arguments made here consistent and cogent? Do the arguments really apply empirically to actual organizations? There is scope for considerable future research into equifinality. Such research would include examining different contingencies, different structures, different conceptualizations of performance, and different organizations in different sectors and countries.

An important part of the contingency theory tradition is the differentiation-and-integration approach of Lawrence and Lorsch (1967). This holds that organizations need to differentiate so that each part of an organization fits its subenvironment and tasks and then integrates the different parts sufficiently to achieve the required degree of coordinated action. A way to achieve the required differentiation and integration is to separate the organization into divisions structurally, each with its own structure and objectives, and to have the divisions integrated by a top management team. In this way, the organization is said to be ambidextrous. Tushman, O'Reilly, and their colleagues have energetically pursued this important development of contingency theory.

In their chapter (chapter 4), Binns and Tushman take the ambidexterity approach further. An organization should differentiate into ambidextrous divisions when one part emphasizes exploration while the other part emphasizes exploitation such that each part requires an appropriate and different structure. But before an organization reaches that position, it must innovate successfully. Based on field research, Binns and Tushman identify traps at the crucial incubation stage of developing ideas for a new business. They go onto recommend how an organization can incubate effectively. This involves rigorous statement of hypotheses and empirical testing. The organization runs experiments of various kinds and generally acts in a way highly conducive to a rational approach. This continues the flavor of rationalism that has long been a hallmark of the classical and contingency approaches to organizational theory. Thus it is in contrast to the institutional theory of organizations that is popular in many quarters of organizational theory research today, which emphasizes myth and ritual.

Qiu and Donaldson (chapter 5) critique the belief that matrix structures in multinational corporations (MNCs) provide two hierarchies and so offer considerably greater information processing than conventional single hierarchies. On the contrary, Qiu and Donaldson argue that matrix structures do not possess multiple hierarchies and so have only a limited advantage over conventional structures.

Matrix organizational structures offer the advantage of superior information processing compared with conventional structures. For example, in a product-geographic matrix, there are managers of the products and managers of the geographies, so the information processing by managers that is available in the matrix is greater than in either the product structure or the geographic structure on their own. Some scholars (Wolf and Egelhoff 2002) go further, arguing that matrix structures are multiple hierarchies and so add together the information processing capacities of the multiple hierarchies. For example, in a product-geographic matrix, its information processing capacity would be that of the product hierarchy *plus* that of the geographic hierarchy. If the product hierarchy had 10 units of information processing capacity and the geographic hierarchy had 11 units of information processing capacity, then the product-geographic matrix would have 21 units of information processing capacity.

This assumes, however, that a matrix is made of two hierarchies. In reality, a matrix is only two structures at a single level in the organization's hierarchy. For example, in a product-geographic matrix, reporting to the CEO there are managers of products and managers of geographies. Thus the information processing of the product managers is augmented by the information processing of the geography managers. But at the next level down, there are only the managers of the various products in the various geographies. And at the level below them is a hierarchy stretching down to the shop floor. Thus being a matrix structure does not mean there are two hierarchies in the organization. There can be only one hierarchy in a matrix structure. The multiple reporting structure exists at only a single level (e.g., the managers of the products in the geographies). Hence the augmentation by the geographic structure of the information processing of the product structure occurs only at a single level in the hierarchy.

Thus while there is an advantage of the matrix structure compared with a single hierarchy, it is only proportional to one out of the number of levels in the organization's hierarchy. For example, if an organization has seven levels in its hierarchy, then, if it became a matrix, the advantage it would have over when it had a single hierarchy (e.g., a product structure) would be only one-seventh. This advantage may still be well worth having, but it is much less than that postulated by the multiple hierarchies model (i.e., doubling of information processing capacity), which sets unrealistic expectations for managers and organizational designers.

The theory of the limited advantage of matrix structures presented by Qiu and Donaldson in this book can be generalized beyond the discussion in their chapter. The structural dimensions involved are not merely the products and the geographies, used here to illustrate the analysis, but also the functional structure. The analysis has also been generalized from the two-dimensional matrix to the three-dimensional matrix. Again, while the data in this chapter were from MNCs, the argument is not restricted to MNCs, but can apply to any organization that features a matrix—providing that the matrix exists at high hierarchical levels, e.g., close under the CEO, as discussed herein.

If the matrix were at a lower hierarchical level, its contribution would be less than at the high level considered here, because the information processing at lower hierarchical levels will tend to be less consequential for decision making than the information processing at the higher hierarchical levels. Therefore, the advantage for a lower-hierarchical-level matrix would exist, but be less than that of a higher-hierarchical-level matrix. Thus, for the lower-hierarchical-level matrix, the matrix advantage would be less than for the higher-hierarchical-level matrix.

Organizations can have matrices at several hierarchical levels simultaneously so that there might be, for example, a matrix at a high hierarchical level (e.g., reporting to CEO), a matrix at mid-hierarchical level (e.g., between an accountant reporting to the chief of finance at head office and to the manager of the plant where the accountant is located), and a matrix at the bottom of the hierarchy (e.g., a scientist in an R&D laboratory reporting to a head of the research project and to the head of the discipline, such as chemistry).

As seen in the chapter by Qiu and Donaldson, for the high-level matrix structure, its advantage over a single-dimensional structure is $1/h$, where h is the number of levels in the hierarchy of the organization. If the matrix is at the level below, its contribution is limited to its part of the organization. If there were nine other units at the same level, the matrix would have a matrix advantage of one-tenth of $1/h$. That is, more generally, the matrix advantage of a unit with u peer units is $1/h \times 1/(u + 1)$. As we descend the hierarchy of an organization, the number of peer units tends to increase so that by the lower level of the hierarchy, the matrix advantage is only about a few percent. Therefore, even if in an organization there were matrix structures at the top, middle, and bottom of the hierarchy, the latter two would add only very small advantages to the advantage from the matrix at the high hierarchical level. Thus the argument that matrix advantages are small holds even if there are matrices not only at the top but also at middle and lower hierarchical levels as well. This supports the generalizability of the conclusion that matrix advantage is limited. It is attained by carrying through the quantitative modeling that has been used on the matrix problem in this book.

This suggests that continued attention to the formal analysis of organizational structures may well be fruitful. Structural aspects of an organization are amenable to mathematical modeling. There is potentially much about the structures of organizations that generalizes across organizational types, countries, and time if we take care to make a formal analysis.

Again, the data used in the chapter by Qiu and Donaldson were of German firms, but the argument should apply also to organizations that are from home countries other than Germany and that are of types of organizations other than firms. However, the generality of these findings cannot be assumed and is a theoretical contention that requires future empirical testing by researchers working on organizations of different types from different countries. Further, the dependent variable in the present analysis of MNCs is internationalization, whereas it would be desirable to extend the dependent variable to organizational performance, for reasons of both generalizability and utility.

Egelhoff and Wolf's chapter (chapter 6) critiques existing organizational theory for its lack of relevance for managers facing practical problems. They argue that this comes from the fragmentation into multiple organization theories that prevent clear, coherent recommendations being made to managers. Egelhoff and Wolf hold that a preferable approach is for the various theories in organizational theory to be reconciled by identifying the differing conditions under which each theory holds true. Then the lower-level theories can be synthesized into a more general theory. Being more comprehensive, this general theory is more likely to be able to offer coherent recommendations to managers, and thus organizational theory can become more practically useful and so more relevant to managers.

The creation of contingency theory was a similar process of taking two organization theories, classical management theory (Brech 1957) and human relations theory (Likert 1961), which differ considerably, and identifying conditions under which each is valid (Burns and Stalker 1961). That is to say, identifying a moderator, e.g., technological and market uncertainty, that determines which theory is valid in each situation. This identification of a moderator led to a more valid and coherent organizational theory: contingency theory. Nevertheless, in the present era, there are many theories apart from contingency theory, such as agency theory (Jensen and Meckling 1976), institutional theory (Meyer and Scott 1983), population ecology (Hannan and Freeman 1977), and transactions costs theory (Williamson 1975), which differ from each other and fragment organizational theory.

Egelhoff and Wolf effectively suggest reuniting contemporary organization theory by subsuming individual organizational theories into a more general theory. They illustrate the prospects for this by considering the different tasks for which hierarchical and network structures are effective. The information processing capacities of different structures are discussed and related to the information processing requirements of different tasks. Cogent recommendations are forthcoming about when to use hierarchical structures and when to use network structures.

Indeed, modern organization theory has sometimes been criticized for being too rich and diverse, in that it is a profusion of paradigms that fragments knowledge and frustrates practitioners seeking advice about practical problems (Donaldson 1995). Egelhoff and Wolf suggest a solution through bringing theories together by specifying the conditions under which each holds true. In the future, a fuller realization of the programmatic visions of Egelhoff and Wolf would be to bring into one framework the contemporary major organizational theories of agency theory, institutional theory, population ecology and transaction costs theory. Donaldson (1995) has already offered some discussion of what would be involved in an empirical integration of these theories. The challenge, in the spirit Egelhoff and Wolf, would be the more ambitious, and very worthwhile, task of forging a *theoretical* integration between these disparate organizational theories. In the present volume, not only have Egelhoff and Wolf pointed the way, but Burton et al. have also made strides in that direction with their contingency theory of contracting, which brings together elements of transactions costs theory within an overall contingency theory framework.

In their chapter (chapter 7), Lok, Hwang, and Höllerer give an appreciation of stewardship theory from the theoretical perspective of institutional theory. Their focus is on the role of management in the capitalist system. They provide a generally critical review of developments in capitalism. As they state, agency theory has provided a theoretical basis for corporate governance in business and other organizations, while stewardship theory has offered an antithesis.

Agency theory sees managers as tending to run the organization so as to maximize their own interests, at cost to the principals—that is, the owners—especially shareholders. These tendencies may be curbed to a degree, however, through controls on the managers, such as through vigilant monitoring by boards of non-executive directors and through financial incentives for managers. To the contrary, stewardship theory sees managers as tending to run organizations so as to maximize the performance of the organization and thereby benefit shareholders and other stakeholders. This involves intrinsic motivations of managers, through their empowerment, which is increased by managers being executive directors and reducing the controls on them. In contrast, the increased controls stipulated by agency theory tend to undermine the intrinsic motivation of managers.

The debate between agency theory and stewardship theory has often been pursued in a positivist and functionalist theoretical framework by seeking to see which set of corporate governance practices offers the higher organizational performance (e.g., whether economic returns to shareholders are superior from non-executive directors or executive directors, Baysinger and Butler 1985). However, Lok et al. distance themselves from this kind of analysis and instead argue for a more social constructionist theoretical approach. In this, the significance of theories is more the way they shape thinking and hence offer legitimated models to be turned into practice. Lok et al. hail stewardship theory as playing this kind of role and as, therefore, being an ethico-political movement.

Regarding the future of stewardship theory, Lok et al. note that its influence is far less than that of its antithesis, agency theory, as measured by the citations for stewardship theory being far fewer than those of agency theory. This suggests that there may be scope for work to extend and broaden stewardship theory research so that it has greater influence in the future.

Lok et al. see stewardship theory as providing a more micro-level analysis of the role of the manager. And they see the resultant model as being consistent with corporate responsibility or responsible capitalism. The idea of a coming together of thinking about corporate responsibility and responsible capitalism with thinking about stewardship theory is to be welcomed.

Many of the maladies that afflict contemporary society have the underlying defect that they encourage a pathological emphasis on the pursuit of profits. This is evident in the banking scandal (the "Global Financial Crisis"), which was underlain at the micro-level by the heightened emphasis on incentive pay linked to firm profits in the roles of the CEO and managers. These are the sort of controls on managers specified in agency theory, whose negative effects are specified in stewardship theory. Hence stewardship theory could be a micro-level analysis of responsible capitalism.

As Weber (1968) advised, however, modern organizations possess many similar characteristics, such as bureaucratic organization, across both capitalist and non-capitalist organizations. Similarly, many maladies of contemporary organizations do not lie in capitalism, because many of these organizations are not owned by anyone. Hence, in such organizations, there are no owners sitting atop the hierarchy pressurizing the lower-level members of the organization for greater profits and the like. Nevertheless, the staff members are pressurized by their managers to perform in ways defined by their superiors.

At the heart of the matter lies the syndrome, so ably described by Lok et al., that the senior managers lack trust in their more junior colleagues to do a good job. This could be because the seniors think the juniors lack the necessary motivation and commitment or because the seniors think the juniors lack ability, or have divergent interests. Therefore, the seniors may monitor their junior colleagues increasingly closely, set goals for them, and check on their performance with increasing detail and frequency.

The remedy for such organizations is for them to become organizations in which individual employees below the organization's board of directors have more rather than less authority to set their own goals and to take what actions they deem best, consistent with the contingencies. The goals they set for themselves need to attend both to economic necessities, such as providing acceptable returns, and also to value-based and ethical precepts.

Hopefully, this brief discussion may encourage the reader to think about how, in future research, the micro analysis of stewardship theory may help flesh out the macro analysis of "responsible capitalism"—with the proviso that the macro analysis may not be restricted to organizations whose problems stem from their capitalist nature.

Organizational theory is advancing. Research continues to grow and investigate more aspects of organizations. Contingency theory research has extended to study multiple misfits, contingency imperatives despite multiple contingencies, and economic contracting, as examples.

Academic colleagues conducting this research span continents and generations. It is particularly pleasing to see younger scholars contributing to this book.

Organizational theory suffers from a profusion of theoretical paradigms. Yet there is the encouraging future prospect, held out in this book, of bringing together disparate organizational theories in a high-level contingency theory that would identify the conceptual position in which each theory is valid.

Moreover, a more unified field of organizational research, across various theories and topics, is more plausible given that there are underlying commonalities in empirical research methods. These methods include, but are not restricted to, the search for associations between variables and the control of extraneous causes. These are conspicuous in quantitatively oriented organizational research, but even qualitative research methods often use frequency counts and the like. This commonality of research practice helps to make research from different theories more mutually intelligible and reduces, somewhat, paradigm incommensurability.

The development of theory, however, rightly remains a fundamental objective in organizational research.

It is gratifying to see the contributors to this volume taking a decidedly scientific approach.

Adherence to the scientific method will advance organizational theory research in the years to come.

References

Baysinger, B. D. and H. N. Butler. 1985. Corporate governance and the board of directors: Performance effects of changes in board composition. *Journal of Law, Economics and Organization* 1:101–24.

Brech, E. F. L. 1957. *Organisation: The framework of management.* London: Longmans, Green.

Burns, T. and G. M. Stalker. 1961. *The management of innovation.* London, UK: Tavistock.

Burton, R. M. and B. Obel. 1998. *Strategic organizational diagnosis and design: Developing theory for application.* Boston, MA: Kluwer Academic Publishers.

Child, J. 1972. Organizational, environment and performance: The role of strategic choice. *Sociology* 6:1–22.

Child, J. 1977. Organizational design and performance: Contingency theory and beyond. *Organization and Administrative Sciences* 8:169–83.

Child, J. 1984. *Organization: A guide to problems and practice.* London, UK: Harper and Row.

Davis, J. H., F. D. Schoorman, and L. Donaldson. 1997. Toward a stewardship theory of management. *Academy of Management Review* 22:20–47.

Donaldson, L. 1995. *American anti-management theories of organization: A critique of paradigm proliferation.* Cambridge: Cambridge University Press.

Donaldson, L. 1996. *For positivist organization theory: Proving the hard core.* London: Sage.

Donaldson, L. 2001. *The contingency theory of organizations.* Thousand Oaks, CA: Sage.

Doty, D. H., W. H. Glick, and G. P. Huber. 1993. Fit, equifinality, and organizational effectiveness: A test of two configurational theories. *Academy of Management Journal* 36:1196–1250.

Gresov, C. and R. Drazin. 1997. Equifinality: Functional equivalence in organization design. *Academy of Management Review* 22:403–28.

Hannan, M. T. and J. Freeman. 1977. The population ecology of organizations. *American Journal of Sociology* 82:929–64.

Jensen, M. C. and W. H. Meckling. 1976. Theory of the firm: Managerial behaviour, agency costs and ownership structure. *Journal of Financial Economics* 3:305–60.

Lawrence, P. R. and J. W. Lorsch. 1967. Differentiation and integration in complex organizations. *Administrative Science Quarterly* 12:1–47.

Likert, R. 1961. *New patterns of management.* New York: McGraw-Hill.

Meyer, J. W. and W. R. Scott, with the assistance of B. Rowan and T. E. Deal. 1983. *Organizational environments: Ritual and rationality.* Beverly Hills, CA: Sage.

Weber, M. 1968. *Economy and society: An outline of interpretive sociology.* Roth, G. and C. Wittich, eds. New York: Bedminster Press.

Williamson, O. E. 1975. *Markets and hierarchies: Analysis and antitrust implications, a study in the economics of internal organization.* New York: Free Press.

Wolf, J. and Egelhoff, W. G. 2002. Research notes and commentaries: A reexamination and extension of international strategy-structure theory. *Strategic Management Journal* 23 (2):181–89.

Index